How to Buy the Right Used Car

Your easy and complete how to guide

Stephen Turvil

Copyright Notice

ISBN: 9798645889470

Disclaimer

How to Buy the Right Used Car presents information only. It is not warranted to be free of errors and/or omissions. Readers that apply the information in any context do so of their own volition and take full responsibility for any consequences. The author disclaims any liability for any loss, damage, injury, and/or disruption of any kind however – and to whomsoever – it may occur.

Introduction

How to Buy the Right Used Car walks you through the process in easy to follow steps. On this basis:

- Check List 1: Lifestyle Requirements confirms what characteristics the car must have to meet your needs

- Check List 2: Home Appraisal helps you provisionally assess the car from its advert before travelling to see it in person

- Check List 3: Paperwork reveals how to check the car's service history, invoices, and any other documents

- Check List 4: Vehicle Inspection explains how to spot a wide range of faults

- Check List 5: Make the Deal gives you the tools, confidence, and attitude to negotiate tremendous terms of sale.

Check List 1:

Lifestyle Requirements

Check List 1: Lifestyle Requirements

Contents

Check List 1, as mentioned, helps you establish what characteristics the vehicle must have to be suitable. It includes:

- Factor 1: Class
- Factor 2: Power Source
- Factor 3: Transmission
- Factor 4: Drive
- Factor 5: Equipment
- Factor 6: Things to Avoid
- Factor 7: Price
- Factor 8: Age
- Factor 9: Mileage
- Factor 10: Service History
- Factor 11: Place of Sale
- Factor 12: Sourcing
- Conclusion

Check List 1: Lifestyle Requirements

Factor 1: Class

To get started, list below in the space provided any class of vehicle that suits your lifestyle. First, however, consider the Supporting Material that follows on the next few pages. It will help you make an informed decision.

....

....

....

....

....

....

....

....

....

....

....

....

....

....

....

....

....

....

....

....

....

....

....

....

....

....

....

....

Check List 1: Lifestyle Requirements

Factor 1: Class

Supporting Material

Class is the simple, ever evolving framework that enables your car to be categorised in broad terms. The influencing factors include:

- body style
- size
- ride height
- number of seats
- prestige
- capability off road.

The following paragraphs reveal the purpose, strengths, and weaknesses of a representative, purely theoretical car of each class. This information gives you an overview of the market.

City

The city car's purpose is to be a cheap, entry level workhorse that best suits the urban environment. Strengths include its compact proportions, good visibility, and tight turning circle that make it easy to manoeuvre on small roads. Its weaknesses include the lack of space and refinement that make longer trips tedious. This example car's specification is:

- size: 3.6 metres long by 1.7 metres wide
- body style: hatchback
- doors: 2
- seats: 5
- engine: 1.0 litre, 60 horsepower, petrol
- transmission: 5-speed manual

- cargo capacity: 230 litres
- driven wheels: front.

Note: Also available with 4 doors. This option makes it easier to access the rear seats which is great if you have passengers.

Supermini

The supermini's purpose is to inherit strengths from its smaller, city class sibling and add refinement. It has much less of a budget feel. It therefore better suits longer, faster journeys on bigger roads such as motorways. Limited cabin space is its main drawback. This example car's specification is:

- size: 4.0 metres long by 1.7 metres wide
- body style: hatchback
- doors: 4
- seats: 5
- engine: 1.2 litre, 70 horsepower, petrol
- transmission: 5-speed manual
- cargo capacity: 290 litres
- driven wheels: front.

Note: Also available with 2 doors. This configuration creates a sportier look at the expense of easy access to the rear seats.

Small Family

The car's purpose is to be big enough for a family, yet small enough to manoeuvre easily in busy towns and cities. Key strengths include its practicality, versatility, and modest running costs. What a winning combination. On the downside, it is a head over heart buy. This example car's specification is:

- size: 4.3 metres long by 1.8 metres wide
- body style: hatchback

- doors: 4
- seats: 5
- engine: 1.4 litre, 100 horsepower, petrol
- transmission: 5-speed manual
- cargo capacity: 370 litres
- driven wheels: front.

Note: Also available in estate form. Expect a larger boot and a squarer rear roof that make it easier to pack awkward, boxy items such as furniture. The flat, slide in load edge above the rear bumper facilitates too. In contrast, the 2 door version sacrifices family friendly features in favour of sportier styling.

Large Family

The vehicle's purpose is to inherit strengths from its small, family class bedfellow then add more space, refinement, and prestige. But it is not all advantage. The extra bulk means it best suits large roads where it has room to stretch its legs. In contrast, it feels cumbersome in town and it cannot squeeze into small parking spaces. This example car's specification is:

- size: 4.8 metres long by 1.8 metres wide
- body style: hatchback
- doors: 4
- seats: 5
- engine: 1.8 litre, 140 horsepower, diesel
- transmission: 6-speed manual
- cargo capacity: 530 litres
- driven wheels: front.

Note: Also available in estate form.

Compact Executive

The vehicle's purpose is to be a prestigious, fashionable

lifestyle statement. It therefore comes in saloon form to draw faint (very, very faint) comparison with some of the most luxurious and prestigious cars in the world. It has sporty handling, too. As for the negatives, the boot is somewhat shallow and the tailgate is small so it cannot take luggage that fits easily into a hatchback. This example car's specification is:

- size: 4.7 metres long by 1.8 metres wide
- body style: saloon
- doors: 4
- seats: 5
- engine: 2.0 litre, 150 horsepower, diesel
- transmission: 6-speed manual
- cargo capacity: 480 litres
- driven wheels: rear.

Note: Also available in estate form.

Medium Executive

See Compact Executive for the overview but expect more space, prestige and refinement. This example car's specification is:

- size: 4.9 metres long by 1.8 metres wide
- body style: saloon
- doors: 4
- seats: 5
- engine: 2.0 litre, 190 horsepower, diesel
- transmission: 6-speed automatic
- cargo capacity: 530 litres
- driven wheels: rear.

Note: Also available in estate form.

Large Executive

The car's purpose is to be extremely luxurious and extremely prestigious. It is a step up on the medium executive. It therefore only comes in saloon form to emphasise its high status. An estate option would be beneath it. This lifestyle statement is for cruising effortlessly to the golf club not taking rubbish to the recycling centre. It also has a space age equipment specification. On the downside, its sheer bulk makes it a handful on small roads and if its countless gadgets fail they cost a lot to repair. This example car's specification is:

- size: 5.1 metres long by 1.9 metres wide
- body style: saloon
- doors: 4
- seats: 5
- engine: 3.0 litre, 250 horsepower, diesel
- transmission: 8-speed automatic
- cargo capacity: 510 litres
- driven wheels: rear.

Ultra Luxury Saloon

The ultra luxury saloon is the most cosseting car on the planet. That is its reason for being. On this basis, the carpet is sumptuously thick and there is a fridge for champagne. There are also downsides. It constantly gets attention, costs more to run than a small country, and it needs a parking bay the size of a football pitch. Furthermore, its size ensures that the handling is best appreciated from the back seats. Best leave the driving to your chauffeur. This example car's specification is:

- size: 5.6 metres long by 2.0 metres wide
- body style: saloon

- doors: 4
- seats: 5
- engine: 6.75 litre, 540 horsepower, petrol
- transmission: 8-speed automatic
- cargo capacity: 460 litres
- driven wheels: rear.

Compact Multipurpose

The car's purpose is to be small, easy to manoeuvre, and cheap to run yet spacious for its size. Its proportions therefore match the supermini but it has a taller, boxier body that maximises headroom. Furthermore, the square rear roof lets it easily swallow large, boxy cargo and the seats slide, fold, and bend to facilitate further. Fold the passenger seat flat, for example. Or is it better to move the rear bench forward? What a pity the handling is dull. This example car's specification is:

- size: 4.0 metres long by 1.7 metres wide
- body style: tall, van-like, estate
- doors: 4
- seats: 5
- engine: 1.0 litre, 100 horsepower, petrol
- transmission: 5-speed manual
- cargo capacity: 320 litres
- driven wheels: front.

Medium Multipurpose

See Compact Multipurpose for context. In contrast, it is family size and more refined. This example vehicle's specification is:

- size: 4.4 metres long by 1.8 metres wide
- body style: tall, van-like, estate
- doors: 4

- seats: 5
- engine: 1.6 litre, 110 horsepower, petrol
- transmission: 6-speed manual
- cargo capacity: 430 litres
- driven wheels: front.

Large Multipurpose

See Compact and Medium Multipurpose for the overview. However, the vehicle is larger and has 7 seats. The third row emerge from the floor of the boot as needed. This example car’s specification is:

- size: 4.8 metres long by 1.9 metres wide
- body style: tall, van-like, estate
- doors: 4
- seats: 7
- engine: 2.0 litre, 140 horsepower, diesel
- transmission: 6-speed manual
- cargo capacity: 300 litres
- driven wheels: front.

Compact Sports Utility

The vehicle's purpose is to excel on extreme, off road terrain yet be small enough to manoeuvre easily through congested cities. Strengths include high ground clearance that help it leap over logs, rocks, and spare copies of this book. Furthermore, it has special off road features such as a system that optimises the response of the throttle, transmission, and traction control to suit the terrain. Choose sand mode, for example. Downsides include its complex design. There is a lot to break and how many off road features do you really need? It is annoying to fix these components if the toughest hazard you face is artificial grass. This example car’s specification is:

- size: 4.4 metres long by 1.8 metres wide
- body style: muscular, tall and boxy
- doors: 4
- seats: 5
- engine: 1.6 litre, 120 horsepower, diesel
- transmission: 6-speed manual
- cargo capacity: 350 litres
- driven wheels: front and rear.

Medium Sports Utility

See Compact Sports Utility for the overview. However, it is larger and more refined. This example car's specification is:

- size: 4.6 metres long by 1.9 metres wide
- body style: muscular, tall and boxy
- doors: 4
- seats: 5
- engine: 2.0 litre, 150 horsepower, diesel
- transmission: 6-speed manual
- cargo capacity: 420 litres
- driven wheels: front and rear.

Large Sports Utility

See Compact and Medium Sports Utility. In addition, expect more space and a premium ambiance. This example car's specification is:

- size: 5.0 metres long by 2.0 metres wide
- body style: muscular, tall and boxy
- doors: 4
- seats: 5
- engine: 2.0 litre, 250 horsepower, diesel
- transmission: 8-speed automatic

- cargo capacity: 520 litres
- driven wheels: front and rear.

Compact Crossover

The vehicle's purpose is to inherit the popular, fashionable styling of the compact sports utility but forgo most of the extreme off road features that increase cost. It is the bridge between traditional car and sports utility. Strengths include the muscular look and high ride height. The latter helps off road. As for negatives, the vehicle arguably feels fake as the rugged styling promises off road capability that is not forthcoming. That is a pity. This example car's specification is:

- size: 4.2 metres long by 1.8 metres wide
- body style: muscular, tall and boxy
- doors: 4
- seats: 5
- engine: 1.6 litre, 120 horsepower, petrol
- transmission: 6-speed manual
- cargo capacity: 350 litres
- driven wheels: front.

Medium Crossover

See Compact Crossover. However, it is family size, more refined, and better equipped. This example car's specification is:

- size: 4.4 metres long by 1.8 metres wide
- body style: muscular, tall and boxy
- doors: 4
- seats: 5
- engine: 2.0 litre, 140 horsepower, petrol
- transmission: 6-speed manual
- cargo capacity: 430 litres
- driven wheels: front.

Large Crossover

See Compact and Medium Crossover but expect more space, sophistication, and prestige. This example car's specification is:

- size: 4.7 metres long by 1.8 metres wide
- body style: muscular, tall and boxy
- doors: 4
- seats: 5
- engine: 2.0 litre, 170 horsepower, diesel
- transmission: 6-speed manual
- cargo capacity: 565 litres
- driven wheels: front.

Sports Coupé

The sports coupé's purpose is to be fun and the confident handling, potent engine, and sense of occasion ensure it succeeds. On the downside, it sits low to the ground which makes it tricky to get in and out. The ride is firm, too. Also, style is more important than practicality so it is more weekend toy than everyday workhorse. There is very little room for luggage, for example. This example vehicle's specification is:

- size: 4.2 metres long by 1.8 metres wide
- body style: coupé
- doors: 2
- seats: 2
- engine: 2.0 litre, 200 horsepower, petrol
- transmission: 6-speed manual
- cargo capacity: 230 litres
- driven wheels: rear.

Note: Also available in convertible form. The benefit is that you bask in the sun and have a more intense drive. That said, the roof is more likely to leak and - if open - it cannot stop debris entering the cabin if you crash. Finally, you have to tolerate wind noise, bird mess on the seats, and a lack of privacy.

Grand Tourer Coupé

The grand tourer's purpose is to be fast, sporty, and thrilling yet supremely comfortable over a very, very long distance. In other words, it perfectly balances handling and comfort. What better car for cruising across continents in style? The weakness is that it attracts attention that is not always wanted. Can you accept that? This example car's specification is:

- size: 4.8 metres long by 1.9 metres wide
- body style: coupé
- doors: 2
- seats: 2
- engine: 6.0 litre, 500 horsepower, petrol
- transmission: 8-speed automatic
- cargo capacity: 300 litres
- driven wheels: rear.

Note: Also available in convertible form.

Supercar

The supercar's purpose is to be fierce, amazingly fast, and so frightening you call for mother. Expect 200 miles per hour and remarkable handling. The negative is that you have to be exceptionally talented behind the wheel to fully exploit its potential. It is also quick to punish mistakes and repairs cost more than a Hollywood divorce. This example car's specification is:

- size: 4.6 metres long by 2.0 metres wide
- body style: coupé

- doors: 2
- seats: 2
- engine: 4.0 litre, 680 horsepower, petrol
- transmission: 7-speed automatic
- cargo capacity: 250 litres
- driven wheels: front and rear.

Note: Also available in convertible form.

Check List 1: Lifestyle Requirements

Factor 2: Power Source

Consider the Supporting Material that follows then mark on the list any favoured power source. Pick from:

- petrol
- diesel
- electric battery
- hybrid
- plug-in hybrid
- electric hydrogen
- petrol and liquefied petroleum gas.

Check List 1: Lifestyle Requirements

Factor 2: Power Source

Supporting Material

Imagine a fleet of cars parked on a forecourt. Each has its own, unique power source that produces 150 brake horsepower. In every other respect the vehicles match. Even their fluffy dice have the same pattern. This scenario expanded below helps you recognise the typical characteristics, strengths, and weaknesses of each power source and make comparisons. You can then pick favourites.

Vehicle A: Petrol

Vehicle A has an internal combustion engine that is fuelled by petrol. The petrol is stored in a tank and there is enough to cover up to 400 miles. In addition, the car is supported by a vast network of fuel stations and it can be topped up in minutes. Such strengths are a contrast to some alternative power sources. Furthermore, there is plenty of expertise among mechanics to fix faults. Petrol, after all, is not a new and unknown power source that is likely to confuse. That is handy. It is not in your interest to own a car that is hard to fix.

However, life is not perfect behind the wheel of the petrol vehicle. Why? Because it burns fossil fuel which is a limited, expensive to procure resource. Furthermore, it expels pollution via its exhaust which is bad for the planet and your health. Note too that the car averages 50 miles per gallon in laboratory tests.

Vehicle B: Diesel

Vehicle B has an internal combustion engine that is powered by diesel. Like the petrol vehicle, the range is 400 miles per tank and it can be refuelled anywhere quickly. It is also widely understood by mechanics and pollutes through its exhaust. However, in contrast to the petrol it averages 65 miles per gallon rather than 50. The engine also has more torque (turning power) so it pulls better while spinning slowly. At 1,500 revolutions per minute, for instance. This ensures it requires fewer gear changes.

There are also downsides compared to the petrol. Whereas each case has to be considered individually, conventional wisdom is that some faults cost more to repair. Furthermore, the engine makes a less pleasing, arguably intrusive, rattling noise that you might not like.

Vehicle B also has a diesel particulate filter to minimise its impact on the environment. This filter has to be cleaned or it becomes saturated by the pollution it catches. The engine then struggles for power. In theory, the filter cleans itself as you drive but this might not be sufficient if you typically make short, low speed trips in town. Fast blasts on the motorway more effectively clean the filter. Do you use motorways regularly?

Furthermore, there is a tank in the vehicle that contains AdBlue. This combination of water and urea is fired into the exhaust stream to neutralise nitrogen oxides. The tank only contains so much, of course. It therefore has to be topped up every few thousand miles. That is a cost and a hassle. In addition, if the AdBlue tank is empty you cannot ignore the related warning on the dashboard. The car refuses to start without AdBlue. Never fear, though. It will not stop in the middle of a journey if the tank runs dry. The only problem is restarting.

Vehicle C: Electric Battery

Vehicle C incorporates an electric motor that is powered by a battery. On this basis, it cannot burn petrol or diesel then pollute the planet. That is its strength. However, the battery is charged by electricity that might be produced by burning fossil fuel at a power station. Best therefore perceive this car as saintly but not completely guilt free. It is low fat not zero.

Furthermore, the maximum range is 200 miles per charge. That is significantly less than the petrol and diesel cars manage per tank. In addition, like the aforementioned counterparts the range is influenced by driving style, what equipment is running, and traffic. Low temperature plays a role, too. You might therefore have a far shorter, real world range than the publicised maximum particularly through the the winter. Might this limited range compromise your lifestyle?

Now consider longevity. A new laptop battery lets you surf the internet for hours. However, its performance diminishes with use until you can only visit a few sites per charge. Much the same applies to the car so its range falls over time. It might fall a lot. What a contrast to the petrol and diesel cars that cover the same distance whether new or old (assuming no faults).

This hassle can be minimised by buying the car but leasing its battery. The manufacturer then has to repair or replace the battery if its performance diminishes too far. Leasing is not necessarily desirable, though. The cost might rise considerably and you have to keep paying. What is the alternative? Also, consider trying to sell the car to somebody else in the future. Who wants an elderly battery or compulsory lease payments?

Charging is tiresome too. Why? Because the vehicle has to be connected to a power source via a cable for a long time. Options include a standard socket that can power any household item. The charge time is measured in ice ages. A manufacture supplied home charger is faster but still takes forever. The quickest option is a fast public charger. Expect an 80 percent charge in about half an hour as a best case scenario. This assumes that you can find such a charger, that it works, and that it is not already in use.

Vehicle D: Hybrid

Vehicle D has an internal combustion engine and an electric motor. The former is powered by petrol and the latter by a battery. The engine ensures the car matches the range of its petrol and diesel counterparts. It can also be refuelled quickly in any town. Furthermore, the electric motor propels the car single-handed for a short time if its power consumption is low. If cruising slowly in town, for example. In this scenario, it cannot burn through your expensive petrol. In addition, the engine starts automatically if the battery is low or you need extra power. Recognise also that the engine charges the battery.

There are downsides too. Consider the cars that only have a combustion engine. What might go wrong? Quite a bit, in fact. Now consider the electric car. It has different parts to break and empty your wallet. So what about the hybrid? It has parts from both and others that make them work together. There is clearly a lot to fail. In addition, whereas hybrid technology is not new most cars only have a petrol or diesel engine. Hybrid is therefore more likely to challenge your mechanic. Challenge equates to cost.

Vehicle E: Plug-in Hybrid

Vehicle E has an internal combustion engine and a motor. The former is powered by petrol and the latter by its battery. Note that the vehicle's purpose is to improve upon the hybrid. As such, the battery can be recharged by the engine or in the same manner as the electric car's. Through a standard socket, for example. The latter is far preferable if you want to save money. You might virtually eliminate your use of petrol if you only make short, low energy trips through town. As with the hybrid, the downside is complexity and the comparative lack of experience among mechanics.

Vehicle F: Electric Hydrogen

Vehicle F has a hydrogen powered electric motor. On this basis, the refuelling process is similar to the petrol and diesel cars. So is the range per tank. In contrast, it only emits water vapour so it cannot pollute at the point of use. That is a key strength. Furthermore, hydrogen can be produced from easily replaced materials such as sewage. In contrast, crude oil for fossil fuel takes countless years to form naturally. On the downside, there are only a few hydrogen fuel stations in the world.

Vehicle G: Petrol and Liquefied Petroleum Gas

Vehicle G has an internal combustion engine that is fuelled by petrol and liquefied petroleum gas (LPG). Expect twin fuel tanks, twin fuel gauges, and twin fuel filler flaps. Note too that the gas system is an after market extra that theoretically reduces running costs. Gas, after all, is cheaper than petrol. Typically, the engine burns petrol as it warms up then it swaps to gas. It then reverts back to petrol once the gas tank is empty.

Best consider the negatives, too. Gas is harder to find than petrol, diesel, or good service at a supermarket. Furthermore, any saving that arises from buying less petrol has to be balanced against the cost of maintaining, fixing, and replacing the extra components. Now consider selling the car in the future. A fuel system that only a few people recognise is unlikely to facilitate.

Check List 1: Lifestyle Requirements

Factor 3: Transmission

Consider the Supporting Material that follows, then mark on the list any favoured transmission. Pick from:

- manual
- automatic
- automatic paddle shift.

Check List 1: Lifestyle Requirements

Factor 3: Transmission

Supporting Material

Transmission transfers power from the engine and/or motor to the wheels which is handy if you want to move. Once again, imagine a fleet of cars on a forecourt. Each is identical apart from its transmission. This scenario expanded below enables you to recognise the typical characteristics, pros, and cons of each transmission and make comparisons. You can then choose what suits.

Vehicle A: Manual Transmission

Vehicle A is a manual. The transmission therefore connects and disconnects to the engine via a clutch that you operate with a pedal. Simply press the pedal to separate the engine and transmission, choose a gear, then release the pedal. This configuration has its strengths. Changing gear is fun on an entertaining road, for instance. You also have total control of the selection. On the downside, manual transmission is labour intensive particularly in heavy traffic. Mastering it takes work too. If, therefore, you have bad clutch control or choose the wrong gear the car hops down the road like a kangaroo (or stalls).

Vehicle B: Automatic Transmission

Vehicle B is a modern automatic which makes it easier to drive than the manual. There is no clutch pedal, for starters. Simply press and hold the brake pedal, move the lever to D for drive, then release the brakes. The car now reaches and maintains a fast jogging pace. When more speed is required, press the throttle and the transmission picks the gear that suits your scenario. Gear 6 for motorway cruising, for instance. Also:

- P is park, i.e. transmission locked so the car cannot move
- N is neutral, i.e. no gear selected
- R is reverse, e.g. to show off your parallel parking skills
- S is sport, i.e. improves acceleration by letting the engine spin faster before the transmission changes up.

There is more to consider. If you need a sudden burst of speed press the throttle hard to kick down. This enables the transmission to best interpret your intentions. It then changes, for example, from gear 6 to 3 to facilitate. In contrast, a gradual increase in throttle pressure indicates a comparative lack of urgency. Your transmission might therefore only go from 6 to 5.

Expect manual gear selection too. This is handy. Perhaps the vehicle is rolling down a very long, very steep incline. It therefore accelerates too much, races to top gear, and hits its maximum speed. A low gear limits its speed. Furthermore, it is better to control speed via the gears than to brake for an extended, constant period. If you brake for too long the fluid in the system might boil. It can then be tricky to stop the vehicle.

Manual selection has further benefits. Perhaps the car is struggling to climb a very long, very steep hill while heavily laden. Furthermore, conditions are such that the transmission constantly swaps between 2 and 3. In this scenario, it is easier to maintain momentum by telling the transmission to stay in whatever gear you prefer. Gear 2, perhaps. In the most extreme case, L for low holds the transmission in its lowest gear.

However, the transmission retains some automatic control whatever your input. Perhaps the car is cruising in manually selected top gear at 70 miles per hour. What if you now slow to 5 miles per hour but forget to change down? The car struggles to accelerate, of course. The transmission spots this error then picks a suitable gear. In contrast, selecting a very low gear at high speed is more dangerous than walking into a lion's enclosure dressed as a medium-rare steak. It might send the engine revolutions through the roof, spin the wheels, and force the car into a ditch. The transmission refuses such selections.

Vehicle B with automatic transmission clearly has strengths and weaknesses compared to the manual. It is less labour intensive, for example. It is also impossible to stall or bounce down the road like a kangaroo. Poor gear selection and clutch control cause these issues. On the downside, if you are a sporty driver you might feel disconnected from the car as there is no clutch pedal. This is a common complaint. In addition, the automatic transmission might not always select your favoured gear.

Vehicle C: Automatic Paddle Shift

See Vehicle B: Automatic Transmission. In contrast, manual selection comes via paddles behind the steering wheel rather than a lever. Simply flick the left paddle once to go down a single gear. Flick the right paddle once to move up. The benefit is that you can change gear without taking your hand off the steering wheel.

Interesting Context

Certain classes of vehicle are most associated with a particular type of transmission. A large executive saloon is likely to be automatic, for example. This is because it has to be refined and effortless to drive. It is a cosseting cruiser. In contrast, a sports car that is thrown through corners for fun is likely to be manual.

Check List 1: Lifestyle Requirements

Factor 4: Drive

Consider the Supporting Material that follows, then mark on the list any favoured drive configuration. Pick from:

- front-wheel drive
- rear-wheel drive
- permanent all-wheel drive
- part time all-wheel drive.

Check List 1: Lifestyle Requirements

Factor 4: Drive

Supporting Material

Drive configuration defines which wheels receive power from the engine and/or electric motor. Each type has typical characteristics, strengths, and weaknesses as revealed by the fleet of otherwise identical vehicles discussed below. First, however, note the terms understeer and oversteer. Let us start with the former. Imagine an empty car park that has a big circle painted on its surface. You drive slowly around the circle and keep its circumference between your wheels. The vehicle has no problem performing this task as every tyre has plenty of traction.

However, you now increase speed until the front tyres can no longer stick properly to the tarmac. This ensures the car cannot follow the circumference of the circle irrespective of how far you turn the wheels. It therefore runs wide. It understeers. You might understeer on the road if you corner too fast, hit a slippery patch of tarmac, or forget to tell your friends to buy this book.

Oversteer is more dramatic. Back to the circle, please. Once again, it is easy to keep the circumference between the wheels of the vehicle at low speed. However, as the speed rises the rear tyres struggle for traction. As such, the rear of the car runs wide rather than follow the circumference of the circle. It steers too much. It oversteers. If uncorrected the car might spin.

Vehicle A: Front-wheel Drive

Vehicle A has front-wheel drive so its natural inclination is to understeer if provoked through corners. On this basis, it is arguably safer than a car that is more likely to oversteer. It is typically preferable to run wide than spin. There are negatives too. If you are a sporty driver, you want the front of your vehicle to turn sharply even at high speed. Understeer spoils such fun. However, whereas the vehicle is more inclined to understeer it can also oversteer. These phenomena are not mutually exclusive.

Vehicle A also has a powerful engine so it is more likely to torque steer than some of the alternatives. This includes less powerful front-wheel drive cars. Expect a strong pull on the steering if you accelerate too hard. It pulls left, for example. The classes of car most associated with front-wheel drive are:

- city
- supermini
- small family
- large family
- compact multipurpose
- medium multipurpose
- large multipurpose
- compact crossover
- medium crossover
- large crossover.

Vehicle B: Rear-wheel Drive

Vehicle B has rear-wheel drive so its natural inclination is to oversteer if pushed too hard through the corners. This is not itself a benefit, of course. However, the advantage compared to the front-wheel drive vehicle is the comparative lack of understeer and torque steer that spoil the handling. However, whereas the rear-wheel car is more inclined to oversteer it can understeer. Classes most associated with rear-wheel drive are:

- compact executive
- medium executive

- large executive
- ultra luxury saloon
- sports coupé
- grand tourer coupé
- supercar.

Vehicle C: Permanent All-wheel Drive

Vehicle C has permanent all-wheel drive so fully exploits every bit of traction the surface has to offer. Driven tyres stick better than non driven. This configuration is most helpful off road, in poor weather, and for towing heavy loads. The penalty is that it increases fuel consumption which is bad news for your wallet. There are also more components to break. The classes of vehicle most associated with permanent all-wheel drive are:

- compact sports utility
- medium sports utility
- large sports utility.

Vehicle D: Part Time All-wheel Drive

Vehicle D has part time all-wheel drive so it normally only sends power to the front to save fuel. However, if it struggles for traction the rear wheels come to life. What percentage of power is sent to the rear varies according to the conditions. Expect, for instance, a high percentage if the rear tyres have far more traction than the front. Also, you can lock the vehicle to permanent all-wheel which is handy if it starts to snow. The classes most associated with part time all-wheel drive are:

- compact sports utility
- medium sports utility
- large sports utility
- compact crossover
- medium crossover
- large crossover.

Check List 1: Lifestyle Requirements

Factor 5: Equipment

Consider the Supporting Material that follows, then list in the space provided any equipment the car must have to suit your lifestyle.

Check List 1: Lifestyle Requirements

Factor 5: Equipment

Supporting Material

There are conflicting extremes of thought regarding how much equipment to opt for. The first is to get a car that has little more than a steering wheel and a convenient compartment for travel sweets. The benefit is that there is very little to break. The dashboard is easy to understand, too. The opposite extreme is to pick a car that is bristling with technology and fully embrace the modern era. There is the middle ground too.

Whatever your instinct, consider whether there is any equipment that complements your lifestyle. Do you travel with a dog that struggles in hot weather? If so, air conditioning is essential for its sake. Perhaps alternatively you have a bad arm. Might a powered tailgate make life easier? Or do you have kids that hate travelling? If so, a router that keeps them on the internet might make motoring less stressful. The Appendix at the end of this book summarises what equipment is available and how it typically works. Consult it if necessary.

Check List 1: Lifestyle Requirements

Factor 6: Things to Avoid

Consider the Supporting Material that follows, then list in the space provided any particular features you want to avoid.

Check List 1: Lifestyle Requirements

Factor 6: Things to Avoid

Supporting Material

There are certain characteristics your car could have it is best to avoid. They make it less suitable for you and/or harder to sell to someone else in the future. They might devalue it, too. Consider bright pink paint, for example. You might love it, but most people want something less likely to induce nausea. This is evident by the number of grey cars on the road in comparison. Other characteristics you might like to avoid include:

- taller than your garage
- too long for your driveway
- poor reliability record
- terrible rear visibility
- bad fuel efficiency (for the class and age)
- expensive road tax.

Check List 1: Lifestyle Requirements

Factor 7: Price

Consider the Supporting Material that follows, then note in the space provided how much you plan to spend on your vehicle.

Check List 1: Lifestyle Requirements

Factor 7: Price

Supporting Material

It is important to set a budget. It helps you:

- quickly dismiss cars that are too expensive
- narrow the search criteria
- not spend more than you can afford (or is sensible).

Consider savings first. How much can you take from this total without leaving yourself destitute and/or uncomfortable? If practical, leave enough for a rainy day. Consider too how long it takes to recoup every thousand you spend at the rate you can save. This might influence your decision. You might spend a little more if your savings can be recouped quickly.

In contrast, if the piggy bank is empty see how much you can borrow from a financial institution, family member, or friend. Only borrow what you can repay comfortably which might be less than is offered. On this basis, calculate how much of your monthly income is available for the car loan. The procedure is:

- note your monthly income (after tax)
- subtract existing costs such as home, travel, and food
- deduct a sum for unexpected expenses
- calculate how much is left for a car loan repayment.

Furthermore:

- borrow from a reputable institution or person
- pick a loan that has a low interest rate
- get everything in writing and
- understand the terms (including penalties).

Check List 1: Lifestyle Requirements

Factor 8: Age

Consider the Supporting Material that follows, then note your preferred age range.

Check List 1: Lifestyle Requirements

Factor 8: Age

Supporting Material

Naturally, the car has to be a certain age so consider any preference and what is realistic within your budget. You might want it to be as new as funds permit, for instance. Why not benefit from the latest technology? You might specifically want it new enough to still be covered by the original manufacturer warranty. Alternatively, maybe you want an older vehicle as you prefer the simplicity, style, and feel. Finally, perhaps you favour a particular model that is out of production. If so, establish what years it was produced.

Check List 1: Lifestyle Requirements

Factor 9: Mileage

Consider the Supporting Material that follows, then note any mileage preference in the space provided.

Check List 1: Lifestyle Requirements

Factor 9: Mileage

Supporting Material

Check List 1 Factor 8 helped define what age of vehicle you require. Consider now whether it has to have low, average, or high mileage relative to its age. In the United Kingdom, 10,000 miles per annum is the widely accepted benchmark. If, therefore, you want a 4 year old car that has average mileage expect 40,000 on the clock. In contrast, you might prefer high or low mileage for various reasons. The scenarios below help you clarify what suits.

Vehicle A: Low Mileage

Vehicle A is 5 years old and has 25,000 miles on the clock. It therefore has low mileage relative to its age. This theoretically ensures it is less likely to break than a high mileage counterpart. That is its strength. The penalty is the higher than average price. Whereas it is worth paying extra for low mileage, there is a limit. Why? Because beyond that limit it is easy to source a similar vehicle that is newer. Might that be preferable?

Vehicle B: High Mileage

Vehicle B is 4 years old and has covered 80,000 miles. It therefore has high mileage relative to its age. The obvious downside is the extra wear but this is reflected by a below average price. The latter is the obvious advantage. It might be enough of an advantage to compensate for the condition. Perhaps high mileage is the only factor that brings the car within budget.

Vehicle C: High Mileage

Vehicle C is 1 year old and has 30,000 miles on the clock. That is high for its age but the lower than average price reflects the wear. However, the mileage is still low relative to what the car is capable of throughout its life. It can cover the same distance again many times over. This combination might make it good value for money.

There is further potential advantage if you buy this car but rarely venture far from home. Perhaps you only cover 5,000 miles per annum, for example. That is below average so it counteracts the high mileage the vehicle covered in its first year on the road. In time, this ensures that the high mileage relative to age becomes average. It then becomes low. That is useful. You buy the vehicle for the below average price then perhaps sell years later for above. Note the time frame below:

- year 1: 30,000 (high mileage as average is 10,000)
- year 2: 35,000 (high mileage as average is 20,000)
- year 3: 40,000 (high mileage as average is 30,000)
- year 4: 45,000 (high mileage as average is 40,000)
- year 5: 50,000 (average mileage)
- year 6: 55,000 (low mileage as average is 60,000)
- year 7: 60,000 (low mileage as average is 70,000)
- year 8: 65,000 (low mileage as average is 80,000)
- year 9: 70,000 (low mileage as average is 90,000).

Vehicle D and E: Comparative Wear and Tear

Naturally, wear increases with mileage but the odometer reading only tells part of the story. In other words, fewer miles does not necessarily equate to less wear. Note Vehicle D. It is 5 years old and has 50,000 motorway miles on the clock. Such driving put very little strain on its primary components. The engine revolutions were typically low, very few gear changes were required, and the brake pedal was barely touched.

Vehicle E is the same age but has only covered 40,000 miles (10,000 fewer). However, every mile was in busy, bustling cities not motorways. This city driving more often called for:

- gear changes (clutch and transmission worked harder)
- harsh acceleration (engine worked harder)
- stop and start traffic (brakes worked harder)
- engine turned on and off (starter motor worked harder)
- parking in tight spaces (more blemishes on the paint).

Check List 1: Lifestyle Requirements

Factor 10: Service History

Consider the Supporting Material that follows, then mark on the list any type of service history that is acceptable. Pick from:

- full
- part
- none.

Check List 1: Lifestyle Requirements

Factor 10: Service History

Supporting Material

The vehicle's service history confirms when it was serviced, at what mileages, and by which garages. This work is important as it:

- minimises wear and tear
- reduces the risk of breakdown
- ensures the vehicle is safe
- identifies minor faults before they become serious
- keeps the warranty valid
- slows depreciation
- creates a paper trail that helps verify the mileage.

Consider a comprehensive service. The mechanic first replaces the vehicle's engine oil. Why bother? Because old oil is a less effective lubricant than new. Poor lubrication increases wear and tear. The mechanic also confirms there is enough coolant to stop the engine overheating. If there is not the car might breakdown. It is also important to check the tyres for serious faults that compromise safety. Punctures and bulges, for instance.

Furthermore, the mechanic checks the battery is capable of starting the engine reliably for the foreseeable future. If not, it can be replaced at a convenient time rather than at the point of total failure. This stops the car failing at the side of the road in the middle of the night. The mechanic also inspects and/or services numerous other important components. For instance:

- suspension
- brakes

- lights
- fuel pipes
- wheel alignment
- wheel bearings
- axillary drive belts
- radiator
- clutch
- steering.

There is more to consider. The car might have to be serviced if any warranty is to remain valid. It depends on the terms and conditions. Such work also reduces depreciation, i.e. how much value the vehicle loses per annum. Why? Because for the aforementioned reasons servicing makes it more desirable than unloved counterparts. That is worth a premium. Servicing also creates a paper trail that indicates whether the odometer's reading is correct (mileage). This trail is important as it is unwise to buy a vehicle that is clocked, i.e. mileage reduced to make it look more valuable. The financial penalties can be severe.

Scenarios

The following scenarios provide further insight, points to consider, and help clarify what type of history meets your needs.

Vehicle A: Full Service History

Vehicle A has full service history. As such, its keeper serviced it at the manufacturer recommended intervals from the day it left the factory to now. This was every 10,000 miles or 1 year (whichever came sooner). The car never, ever missed a service and that is as good as it gets. Insist on full history if:

- funds permit
- vehicle is worth a lot of money

- vehicle is relatively new
- vehicle is prestigious, e.g. large executive saloon
- vehicle requires specialist care, e.g. supercar
- vehicle is covered by its manufacturer warranty
- you hope to sell the vehicle easily in the near future.

Vehicle B and C: Part Service History

Vehicle B and Vehicle C have part history so their keepers serviced them, but not as frequently as required. Part history comes in many forms, though. Distinguish, therefore, between horrible gaps that suggest neglect and those that are less troubling. Vehicle B has horrible gaps. Its service history is:

- year 1: service at 10,000 miles
- year 2: service at 20,000 miles
- year 3: service at 30,000 miles
- year 4: missed
- year 5: missed
- year 6: missed
- year 7: missed
- year 8: missed (present day).

As you can see, there was no maintenance whatsoever for the last few years. Perhaps the keeper lacked the inclination, money, or knowledge to care for the car. Whatever the reason, the history fails to inspire confidence. Vehicle C, in contrast, also has part service history but there is less cause for concern. The paperwork states:

- year 1: service at 10,000 miles
- year 2: service at 20,000 miles
- year 3: missed
- year 4: service at 40,000 miles
- year 5: missed

- year 6: service at 60,000 miles
- year 7: missed
- year 8: service at 80,000 miles (present day).

Whereas this history is far from perfect there is evidence of consistent care (albeit too infrequent). The car was not totally neglected for the last few years, for example. Furthermore, it passed through the workshop recently so there is no need to book a service now. Great. That is money saved. Consider part history if:

- limited funds provide no alternative
- vehicle is worth a modest sum
- vehicle is close to the end of its life.

Vehicle D: No Service History

Vehicle D has no service history, so its keeper never serviced it or lost the related paperwork. Only accept this scenario if:

- limited funds provide no alternative
- car is very cheap, old, and only has to last short term.

Check List 1: Lifestyle Requirements

Factor 11: Place of Sale

Consider the Supporting Material that follows, then mark on the list any type of seller that is acceptable. Pick from:

- franchise dealership
- independent dealership
- home dealership
- private seller
- auction.

Check List 1: Lifestyle Requirements

Factor 11: Place of Sale

Supporting Material

Where you buy your car is important as there are cost, warranty, and service implications. Note below the typical characteristics of each type of seller then pick any preference.

Franchise Dealership

The franchise sells a single manufacturer's vehicles, has a prominent site in the community, and a prestigious vibe. It works alongside its manufacturer so sells new cars from the factory in addition to second-hand. Most of the used stock is up to 5 years old. On this basis, the franchise is not the place to find an old banger to last a few months. Furthermore, the salesperson that helps you buy the car and the mechanic that prepares it have detailed, brand specific knowledge that is tricky to find elsewhere. Expect, in other words, any question to be answered correctly and faults to be fixed by a specialist.

Furthermore, the warranty is the remainder of the manufacturer, in-house, new car policy transferred from the last keeper. In other words, you inherit the warranty that came with the car when it was new. This lets the franchise work to its own rules - rather than those of a third party insurer - and pick which parts are covered and for how long. Alternatively expect a new, in-house, used warranty that follows suit, i.e. dealership picks the terms.

Independent Dealership

The independent dealership sells cars from a range of manufacturers, but has no formal association with a particular brand. On this basis, any advice is more independent which can be handy. In addition, the site is smaller and less fancy than the franchise's and the stock is older and less valuable. Note too that the salesperson and mechanic lack the detailed, brand specific knowledge found at the franchise. The warranty options are:

- remainder of the manufacturer, in-house, new car warranty that requires you to take the car to the franchise dealership
- new, in-house, used car warranty that allows the dealership to work to its own rules rather than those of a third party
- third party policy that requires the dealership to follow terms set by its insurer, e.g. told what parts it can fix.

Home Dealership

A single person operates this dealership from a residential address, so there is no formal link to a manufacturer. The stock is from a variety of brands, low value, and there is very little to choose from. The salesperson also works at the kitchen table and the opening hours are erratic. Naturally, there is no well equipped workshop to prepare the car for sale.

The warranty options match the independent dealership. However, how much value is a new, in-house, used car warranty from a home dealership? Imagine knocking on the door months after purchase to explain that your engine exploded. Is the salesperson likely to invite you in or pretend to be on holiday? It is a home address not a forecourt, after all. You cannot wander in off the street and expect to be seen.

Private Seller

The private seller is not running a business and only wants to sell a single car (from home). This ensures it is not prepared by a professional who has a reputation to protect. Neither is there any expectation of a long term relationship. On the plus side, you might be more relaxed chatting to the private seller than a professional trader. The latter knows all the sales tricks.

The warranty options include the remainder of any manufacturer, in-house, new vehicle policy. Alternatively, there is a warranty from a company that has no formal association with any of the vehicle's former suppliers. The seller bought it separately.

Auction

Buying at auction is a big gamble. You might do well or get a worthless pile of junk. Note that prior to purchase you cannot drive the car or even start its engine. That is against the spirit of this book. Furthermore, you are competing with professional traders so it is a tough environment. It is also easy to pay too much for the car if you get excited. The warranty is the remainder of any manufacturer, in-house, new car policy. No warranty whatsoever is the more likely scenario.

Value

There is a final point to consider. The value of your car is partly defined by where it is for sale. Any variation reflects the aforementioned pros and cons. Expect it to be most expensive at the franchise dealership. The descending order is:

- independent dealership
- home dealership
- private
- auction.

Check List 1: Lifestyle Requirements

Factor 12: Sourcing

Consider the Supporting Material that follows, then mark on the list how you plan to find your vehicle. Pick from:

- internet
- local newspaper
- specialist national magazine
- random forecourt visit
- word of mouth.

Check List 1: Lifestyle Requirements

Factor 12: Sourcing

Supporting Material

There are plenty of ways to source a car. The following pages summarise the typical traits of each so you can choose favourites.

Internet

The internet incorporates a vast range of websites that let you search via whatever criteria is important. The highlights include:

- make
- model
- power source
- transmission
- mileage
- colour
- age
- price
- distance from your postcode.

Furthermore, the internet is vast so there is room for sellers to include a significant amount of information and countless pictures. It also lets you pick a garage and view its stock from home. There is no easier way to find and initially evaluate hundreds of cars. The downside is that not every website is up to date. Expect to see listings for cars that have already sold.

Local Newspaper

Your local newspaper costs very little (if anything) and every car is close to home. It also reveals the names, addresses, and phone numbers of garages that might otherwise escape your attention. This alone makes it worth a look. There are downsides, of course. Unlike the internet, there is very little choice of car and not much room for information. Most adverts do not have pictures, for example. Expect the basic facts only.

Specialist National Magazine

The specialist national magazine lists a specific manufacturer's vehicles including classics. It is most helpful if you want something rare and/or loved by enthusiasts. The downsides include:

- very few vehicles for sale
- cars might be hundreds of miles from home
- very little room for information and pictures
- significant competition from enthusiasts
- magazine is only published monthly.

Random Forecourt Visit

The random forecourt visit puts you next to numerous cars simultaneously. You can then learn a lot in a short time. And guess what? You might get lucky. Your perfect car might be there by chance. Now consider the downsides. Travelling can be expensive, time consuming, and tiring.

Word of Mouth

Word of mouth is free. That is its key strength. Simply explain your needs to family, friends, and colleagues then see what happens. Someone might know where a perfect car is waiting. As for negatives, it might take some time to get any feedback and even then it is likely to be vague. For example, your informant might not know whether the car has service history.

Check List 1: Lifestyle Requirements

Conclusion

Congratulations. Check List 1 is complete. Throw a party to celebrate. You now know what characteristics your vehicle must have to be suitable. Now then is the time to find it via the sources you chose above. Perhaps you primarily favour the internet. Once a vehicle has been found proceed to either:

- Check List 2: Home Appraisal if you want to evaluate the vehicle from a distance via its advert
- Check List 3: Paperwork if you plan to immediately see the vehicle in person.

Check List 2:

Home Appraisal

Check List 2: Home Appraisal

Contents

Check List 2 helps you evaluate the car via its advert before travelling to see it in person. Why bother? Because a visit takes time, effort, and money so has to be worth the investment. Before you proceed, have realistic expectations relative to the vehicle's age, mileage, and price. Consider its class too. It is reasonable to be extremely picky if the vehicle is almost new, from a prestigious class, and more expensive than sending your kids to university. Close to perfect is a fair expectation. However, the same cannot be said for an old supermini that is worth less than a politician's promise. Check List 2 incorporates:

- Factor 1: Exterior Damage
- Factor 2: Interior Damage
- Factor 3: Signs of a Hard Life
- Factor 4: Seller Issues
- Factor 5: MOT History
- Factor 6: Missing Information
- Conclusion

Check List 2: Home Appraisal

Factor 1: Exterior Damage

Consider the Supporting Material that follows, then list any exterior damage visible in the photographs.

....
....
....
....
....
....
....
....
....
....
....
....
....
....
....
....
....
....
....
....
....
....
....
....
....
....
....
....
....
....

Check List 2: Home Appraisal

Factor 1: Exterior Damage

Supporting Material

The pictures in the advert reveal whether the car has exterior damage that might empty your wallet quicker than a dodgy casino. Pick a picture to start the inspection. Now pick part of the car that is visible such as the front, right corner and note any imperfection. Now, for example, move your attention from the front, right corner along the length of the vehicle to the rear right corner. Evaluate everything you see. Faults to note include:

- dents
- scratches
- broken lights
- cracked glass
- rust
- faded paint
- scuffed alloy wheels
- broken wheel trim
- bald tyres
- missing components, e.g. door mirrors.

Repeat these steps for any other pictures. Furthermore, consider whether the vehicle is shown from every side. If an important angle is missing the seller might be hiding a fault. He/she might not be, but recognise that your view is impeded. Note too that water and dirt can conceal blemishes. Is the vehicle wet? Is it extremely dirty? In addition, camera flash and sunlight can make a perfect body panel look slightly bent. If you suspect light is distorting the view, evaluate the panel again via another picture.

Check List 2: Home Appraisal

Factor 2: Interior Damage

Consider the Supporting Material that follows, then note any interior damage visible in the photographs.

Check List 2: Home Appraisal

Factor 2: Interior Damage

Supporting Material

Check List 2 Factor 1: Exterior Damage suggested a simple, methodical way to spot faults with the vehicle's exterior via the pictures. Repeat this technique for the interior but look for:

- torn seats
- burst stitches
- cracked leather
- heavy wear
- broken components
- missing components
- stains
- holes for a mobile phone mount
- cigarette burns
- saggy headliner.

Check List 2: Home Appraisal

Factor 3: Signs of a Hard Life

Consider the Supporting Material that follows, then note any evidence of a hard life visible in the photographs.

Check List 2: Home Appraisal

Factor 3: Signs of a Hard Life

Supporting Material

It is important to spot any evidence among the pictures that suggests the car has led a tough life. A hard life equates to above average wear, additional cost, and extra hassle. See below.

Towing

If the car towed it pulled more weight than typical which put further strain on certain components. At the very least the engine, suspension, and transmission worked harder. Can you see a tow bar in the pictures? If present, note any clues that suggest what the vehicle towed. Perhaps it was a very small, very light trailer to the recycling centre once a year. In this scenario there is no extra wear of note. However, maybe it towed a large, heavy caravan half way around the world.

Potential evidence includes club membership stickers. Is there a caravanning sticker in the window? Or are there chocks in the boot that kept a caravan level while parked? Also check for items that suggest it towed a:

- horsebox
- boat
- car, e.g. in relation to banger racing or the motor trade.

It is not necessarily a mistake to purchase the vehicle if it towed. The most likely scenario is that it only did so occasionally. How many of the hundreds of cars you see every day are towing? It is the exception not the rule. However, in the broadest context it is tricky to perceive a tow bar as a positive.

Off Road

If the vehicle ventured off road it battled a tough environment that took no prisoners. Perhaps, for example, it got stuck in water that soaked key electrical items. In addition, maybe it bounced over a rock that broke the exhaust. Warning signs include:

- off road tyres
- winch
- after market underbody protection plates
- tube to help the engine breathe in water
- rock sliders
- poor bodywork.

Police

Be worried if the police used the car. Maybe it leapt over speed bumps while chasing criminals. Perhaps in addition drunk, vomiting party lovers were locked in the rear. Did they try to break out by kicking the doors? Signs of police use include holes in the roof that supported the flashing blue light bar. These holes might be filled with silicon to stop leaks (to hopefully stop leaks). Also check the stereo and interior trim are present. If not, perhaps they were replaced with special equipment to help catch criminals.

Taxi

If the vehicle was a taxi countless passengers climbed onto its rear seats every day. That took a toll on the upholstery. Also consider the starter motor. Why? Because the driver had to repeatedly start the engine then shuffle forward in queues of taxis until it was his/her turn to collect a fare. But how can you tell the car was a taxi? In the United Kingdom, a taxi has a special plate that proves it is allowed to carry paying passengers. Look for remnants of the plate’s mounting in the pictures. Can you see part of a bracket on the front grille? Can you see holes in the rear bumper? Further red flags include:

- citizen band radio antenna
- damage to the paint caused by taxi signs
- blemishes left by the magnetic roof box
- high mileage relative to age
- diesel engine
- no smoking signs
- passenger on the back seat.

Driving School

If the car was used for tuition its engine stalled more than typical. It therefore had to restart frequently which penalised the starter motor. Furthermore, learners had to perfect low speed manoeuvres such as parking, turning in the road, and starting on hills. Such effort took a toll on the clutch (if fitted). Look for:

- dual controls
- marks caused by the magnetic roof box
- blemishes on the paint left by signs
- high mileage relative to age
- type of car favoured by instructors, i.e. tiny and cheap.

Children

The car might be a mess if its keeper had feral kids. Perhaps they bounced on the seats, wrecked the cubbyholes, and rubbed plasticine into the seats. Maybe they then dropped food on the floor, spilt drinks, and got travel sick. Best look for:

- child seats
- marks on the upholstery left by child seats
- small, muddy footprints on the rear of the front seats
- child themed sun blinds

Pets

If the vehicle carried animals it might smell worse than a teenager's bedroom. Note any:

- guard
- crate
- seat cover
- harness
- hair
- toys
- treats
- claw marks where the pet leapt into the boot
- chewed upholstery.

Vast Amount of Luggage

If the car frequently carried tonnes of luggage its interior likely bears the scars. Note the condition of the boot. Is the trim very worn? Is the carpet a mess? Furthermore, check the back of the rear seats. Perhaps the keeper folded them flat to increase capacity then threw paving slabs, rubbish, and other junk on top. Check the roof lining, too. Tall, carelessly placed cargo scuffs.

Driven Hard

If the car was thrashed by a hooligan its engine, transmission, and brakes took a pounding (among other things). This abuse can be hard to spot via the pictures but there is hope. To pick an extreme example, look for stickers such as ‘speed rules’. Club membership stickers and related paraphernalia might provide further insight. Are the members teenagers that do doughnuts in public car parks? Check the internet for evidence. Also, whereas this is a generalisation additions such as a big spoiler tend to be associated with enthusiastic driving.

Check List 2: Home Appraisal

Factor 4: Seller Issues

Consider the Supporting Material that follows, then list any evidence that suggests the seller might be problematic.

Check List 2: Home Appraisal

Factor 4: Seller Issues

Supporting Material

Before you decide whether to see the car in person, note whether it is for sale somewhere you might be happy to purchase. If not, stay home. The following pages suggest how to evaluate the seller.

Dealership

The dealership's website provides insight so have a look. Is it based at a prestigious site in a prime location or a wrecked caravan on wasteland? Naturally, a fancy site does not guarantee good service but it proves the business sells enough cars to afford such a thing. Strong sales suggest it has a reasonable reputation.

Also consider how the site is presented. Is it well maintained and tidy? If the staff cannot be bothered to maintain the site, can they be bothered to source good cars? Can they be bothered to prepare them to a high standard? Can they be bothered to fix post sale issues? A dodgy site implies a sloppy work ethic.

Now consider the stock. It is reassuring to see a reasonable range of cars particularly if most are worth a meaningful amount of money. If there are only a handful of very cheap, very old cars perhaps the business is struggling to find customers. Might the business fail? A warranty from a company that does not exist is no use. Now note the opening hours. Are they conveniently long or by appointment? If the latter, it suggests the site is empty much of the time. That is a worry. Is there anybody there to address any post sale issues?

Private Seller

The private seller is tricky to judge. There is no business website, for starters. However, a name and approximate location might lead to a social media page. Note first the general attitude to life. If the trend is screw the world he/she might be a pain to deal with. Comments such as 'my car broke yet again' provide further insight. The pictures can also be revealing. Is the car pictured with a damp dog on its rear seat?

Auction

Research the auction house online. Also chat to any customers you happen to know, trust, and are not barred from approaching by a restraining order. Auction traits that inspire confidence include:

- comprehensive vehicle descriptions
- clear terms of sale
- purchase guidance
- positive customer reviews
- long established.

Check List 2: Home Appraisal

Factor 5: MOT History

Consider the Supporting Material that follows, then list any MOT issues.

Check List 2: Home Appraisal

Factor 5: MOT History

Supporting Material

In the United Kingdom, the MOT is a legally required inspection that confirms whether the car meets minimum safety and environmental standards. Whether the brakes work, for example. The examiner then issues a pass or fail certificate. The former expires in a year (or slightly longer in some circumstances), and the latter bans the car from the road. It then has to be fixed and retested. Typically, inspection is first required 3 years after registration then annually thereafter. Exceptions include taxis that have to be inspected after 1 year. In contrast, some classics never have to be checked.

If the vehicle is the appropriate age its test results can be seen online. Best do so. This resource provides valuable, independent information that implies whether it is fighting fit or falling apart. Type ‘MOT history’ into a search engine to find the data. Once at the website, simply enter the vehicle’s registration number which is probably visible in the aforementioned photographs. If not, call the seller to ask for it.

Current Certificate

Consider the most recent test result first. When does the certificate expire, for example? Far into the future is clearly preferable. There is then plenty of time before you have to pay for another test and any associated repairs. In addition, if the certificate is new it suggests the vehicle is safe as of now. It is not so easy to be certain if it passed the test months ago.

Alternatively, maybe the certificate is expired or expires soon. Either is a worry. Why? Because it can be hard to find a buyer so a wise seller stacks the odds in his/her favour. A new certificate is enticing so why not arrange a test? Is the car likely to fail?

The certificate might also incorporate a list of minor and/or advisory items, i.e. faults that require attention soon but are not serious enough to fail the test. Note whether any list is long and expensive or short and cheap. Naturally, it is possible the keeper fixed any issues on the day of the test. However, it is sensible to assume such work is outstanding unless proven otherwise. Via receipts you later check in person, for example.

Historic Inspection Results

Historic test results provide further insight. Does the car typically pass or fail inspection? The former is clearly preferable. In addition, is there normally a very long, very expensive list of minor and/or advisory items? Get a feel for the car.

Check List 2: Home Appraisal

Factor 6: Missing Information

Consider the Supporting Material that follows, then list any further information you need before deciding whether to go and see the car.

Check List 2: Home Appraisal

Factor 6: Missing Information

Supporting Material

The advert might exclude information you need before deciding whether to see the car in person. It might alternatively raise some concerns. Naturally, the solution is to contact the seller via the phone and have a quick chat. The potential issues include:

- it is unclear whether the car has a feature you require

- you cannot tell whether there is a dent in the front, right wing or whether the image is distorted by camera flash

- the vehicle has covers that protect its seats but you wonder whether they conceal stains, damage, or excessive wear.

Check List 2: Home Appraisal

Conclusion

Check List 2 is complete. Celebrate via fireworks, music, and an energetic dance that is guaranteed to pull a muscle. Now catch your breath, review any comments you wrote above, and decide whether you want to evaluate the car further in person. Clearly, there is no point proceeding if you have a major concern or too many minor concerns. In contrast, if it is worth further thought:

- call the seller to check the car is still available
- confirm the address
- arrange a time
- check you are insured to test drive, e.g. via a policy you have that is primarily for another car or the seller's policy.

Furthermore, pack anything you might need. For instance:

- this book (Check List 3 is the next step)
- directions to the seller
- pen
- paper
- torch
- gloves
- tyre tread gauge
- soft cloth
- driving licence
- means of payment
- refreshments
- any car you hope to trade-in.

Check List 3:

Paperwork

Check List 3: Paperwork

Contents

Check List 3 explains how to assess the vehicle's paperwork now you have travelled to see it in person. It is sensible to check the paperwork before the car itself. Why? Because however nice the vehicle looks it might be sensible to walk away if the paperwork is problematic. Check List 3 includes:

- Factor 1: V5C Log Book
- Factor 2: MOT Paper Certificates
- Factor 3: Service History
- Factor 4: Invoices
- Factor 5: Background Report
- Factor 6: Clocking
- Factor 7: Manufacturer Recalls
- Conclusion

Check List 3: Paperwork

Factor 1: V5C Log Book

Consider the Supporting Material that follows, then note any problems with the V5C log book.

Check List 3: Paperwork

Factor 1: V5C Log Book

Supporting Material

The V5C log book confirms key facts about the vehicle and facilitates its sale in the United Kingdom. Check first that it is present and genuine. For the latter, hold it to the light and look for watermarks. Ensure too that it relates to the correct car. Does the information it contains match, in other words? Note:

- make
- model
- trim
- power source
- body type
- registration number
- date of registration
- colour.

Furthermore, note the vehicle identification number as written in the log book. Now check it is replicated on the car itself. You can typically find it at the bottom, left corner of the windscreen if viewed from the exterior. Check it digit by digit as the match must be exact. Also note any damage, lack of clarity, or other issue. Issues imply tampering. Tampering can be indicative of theft. If you want further reassurance check the number anywhere else it is on the vehicle. Possible spots include:

- door pillar
- firewall (separates the engine from the cabin)
- wheel well

- floor of the boot
- under a flap of carpet.

In addition, recognise that the log book cannot prove who owns the car. In other words, it cannot prove who has the legal right to sell it. It only names the registered keeper. As this title suggests, the keeper is the person that keeps the vehicle and is responsible for its everyday needs. He/she arranges insurance, for example. Perhaps, therefore, the owner is a company that sells windows and the registered keeper is an employee who travels to see customers.

On this basis, if the car is for sale privately and the keeper claims to be the owner – as is common – ask for proof. The receipt from when he/she bought the vehicle is ideal. Naturally, it is polite to explain why you need to see such documents. Emphasise, for instance, that it says on the log book that it is 'not proof of ownership' so you need reassurance. Best not expect a professional trader to show the receipt, though. He/she bought the vehicle for a trade price which likely makes the current asking price look somewhat high. Purchase from a trusted dealership to minimise your risk.

Check too how many people kept the car up to this point in its life. Is the number reassuring or alarming? Maybe the car is 6 years old and has had 2 keepers. That is fine. Both kept it 3 years on average. But what if 6 people kept it? This implies nobody liked the car enough to keep it more than a year on average. That is troubling so be cautious. Such facts suggest it consistently disappoints its owners. Perhaps it has an intermittent, easy to miss problem which costs a fortune to fix.

Consider too how long the last keeper retained the car. 5 years, maybe. That is encouraging. Nobody keeps a terrible car that long. In contrast, be cautious if it is back on the market after a few weeks. Perhaps in this scenario there is an acceptable explanation such as a change of circumstance. Or is there a fault that is too costly, time consuming, and difficult to repair? Talk to the seller and see if he/she lets anything slip.

Note: In 2006, a significant number of blank log books were stolen and used for unscrupulous purposes. Some might still be in circulation even all these years later. The suspicious serial numbers are BG8229501 to BG9999030 and BI2305501 to BI2800000.

Check List 3: Paperwork

Factor 2: MOT Paper Certificates

Consider the Supporting Material that follows, then list any issues with the paper certificates.

....

....

....

....

....

....

....

....

....

....

....

....

....

....

....

....

....

....

....

....

....

....

....

....

....

....

....

....

....

....

....

Check List 3: Paperwork

Factor 2: MOT Paper Certificates

Supporting Material

Check List 2 Factor 5: MOT History helped you evaluate this information online before travelling to see the vehicle in person. Presumably, therefore, it is satisfactory so there is no need to repeat this step now. However, examiners also issue paper certificates so check that any current certificate is present. It might be handy one day if you cannot immediately access a computer. It is also nice to retain any old certificates.

Check List 3: Paperwork

Factor 3: Service History

Consider the Supporting Material that follows, then note any problems with the vehicle's service history.

Check List 3: Paperwork

Factor 3: Service History

Supporting Material

As mentioned, the car's service history confirms when it was serviced, at what mileages, and by which garages. Look first for a booklet that contains ink stamps. This is the most common way to record the work. Ensure now that the booklet relates to the correct car. Does it contain the appropriate registration number, for example? Be suspicious if such facts are missing, wrong, or obscured. Now think back to Check List 1. It defines what type of history meets your needs. Options are:

- full service history, i.e. vehicle maintained at the intervals recommended by the manufacturer throughout its life

- part service history, i.e. maintained but not as frequently as recommended

- no service history, i.e. never serviced or any evidence of the work is lost.

Naturally, you probably want full or part service history so consider whether the car is satisfactory. But how? First, check how often the manufacturer recommends it is serviced. This is straightforward. Simply refer to the booklet, call the manufacturer, or look online at a credible website. Let us say it is every 10,000 miles or 1 year (whichever is sooner). Now check the first stamp in the service booklet. Is it at 10,000 miles or 1 year? Now note the second ink stamp. Is it at 20,000 miles or 2 years? Repeat the process for the whole history.

However, recognise that the booklet might be entirely fake or contain a few fake ink stamps. Blank booklets can be bought easily. So can ink stamps, so check for evidence of authenticity throughout. This is easy. Simply cross reference the stamps with any accompanying invoices. Do the dates, mileages, and garages match? Whereas this technique cannot prove beyond any doubt that the history is genuine, the seller is unlikely to fake such a wide range of documents. The balance of probability is in your favour.

Alternatively, call the garages that allegedly serviced the vehicle. Now ask for confirmation that it passed through their workshops on the relevant days, at the relevant mileages, and for the relevant reasons. It is polite to explain why. Furthermore, the staff might reveal other information if the conversation flows freely. Maybe the car is known to be problematic. Maybe it is not.

Check List 3: Paperwork

Factor 4: Invoices

Consider the Supporting Material that follows, then jot down any concerns that arise from the invoices.

Check List 3: Paperwork

Factor 4: Invoices

Supporting Material

The invoices reveal how much has been spent maintaining the vehicle, what work has been done, and when. This information has value. Perhaps the invoices confirm it had new brake discs, pads, and tyres throughout in recent weeks. That is significant. It suggests there is no likely short term cost in these areas. In contrast, perhaps the invoices list work required in the near future. Mechanics often add advisory comments. Such facts help you estimate any short term costs.

Now interpret the paperwork further. Perhaps there are a few recent invoices for an intermittent engine fault. How interesting. Maybe the vehicle broke, got repaired, and there is no further cause for concern. However, the number of invoices for the same fault implies it was tricky to fix. Is it fixed, in fact? Alternatively, is the vehicle for sale because its keeper cut his/her loses? If it is now perfect, might the keeper not drive it a while to get value for money? It is hard to be sure but note such information. For this example, pay particular attention to the engine if you later check the car mechanically. Further uses for the invoices include:

- seller claims the vehicle has a new radiator and the accompanying invoice suggests this is true

- seller claims the car has a new timing belt, but suspicious body language and the lack of an invoice suggest otherwise.

Check List 3: Paperwork

Factor 5: Background Report

Consider the Supporting Material that follows, then review the background report and list any issues.

Check List 3: Paperwork

Factor 5: Background Report

Supporting Material

The report comes via an independent company that has no love for you, the seller, or the car. There is no bias, in other words. The report simply states facts and either you or the seller can buy it online. HPI is among the popular suppliers in the United Kingdom. Study the report very, very carefully. Ensure first that it relates to the right car - particularly if the seller bought it. Check the registration matches, for example.

Now confirm the report is up to date. Even weeks old is insufficient as a lot can happen in a short time. Note too whether the car is subject to outstanding finance. If it is, it belongs to the finance provider so it can be repossessed even if you buy it, go home, and consider it yours. Note every other point in the report, too. Examples include whether the car is:

- listed as stolen on a police database (might be stolen but not listed if the keeper has yet to report the crime)
- scrapped
- accompanied by a fraudulent log book
- likely to be clocked (mileage discrepancy)
- exported.

There are further points to note. The company that writes the report might promise to compensate its customer if it wrongly gives the car a clean bill of health. You have to be the customer to benefit, though. If the seller buys the report then shows it to you, the seller is the customer so you are not entitled to compensation. On this basis, maybe get your own report irrespective of anything the seller has. Naturally, pick a supplier that provides as much data as practical as not every report is created equal. The cheapest might not be adequate.

Check List 3: Paperwork

Factor 6: Clocking

Consider the Supporting Material that follows, then note any evidence that suggests the car has been clocked.

Check List 3: Paperwork

Factor 6: Clocking

Supporting Material

If the vehicle is clocked somebody fraudulently lowered the reading on its odometer. He/she lowered the mileage, in other words. Why bother? To make the car appear more valuable. You therefore overpay if you buy it. There is also more wear than indicated so parts have to be replaced sooner than expected. That gets expensive.

Selling the vehicle to someone else in the future is harder, too. An informed motorist might suspect it is clocked and walk away. It is impossible to be totally confident the mileage is correct but the paperwork implies authenticity (or not). The key is to cross reference every document, look for inconsistencies, and note any repairs the car required up to this point in its life. Vehicles A to D below suggest what to look for.

Vehicle A

Vehicle A's MOT, service, and invoice history follow below. Every bit of paper from the moment it left the factory to now is included. Read it and note the following comments. The paperwork says:

- January 2014: new (0 miles)
- August 2014: invoice 1, puncture (4,394)
- January 2015: service 1 (10,112)
- August 2015: invoice 2, brake bulb (14,777)
- January 2016: service 2 (20,632)
- August 2016: invoice 3, tyres (25,947)
- January 2017: MOT 1 (30,282)

- February 2017: service 3 (31,502)
- August 2017: invoice 4, discs and pads (35,947)
- September 2017: invoice 5, headlamp bulb (37,000)
- January 2018: MOT 2 (40,828)
- February 2018: service 4 (41,211)
- January 2019: MOT 3 (50,223)
- February 2019: service 5 (51,124)
- August 2019: invoice 6, all new tyres (55,947)
- September 2019: invoice 7, air con gas (56,800)
- January 2020: MOT 4 (60,222)
- February 2020: service 6 (61,001)
- March 2020: invoice 8, puncture (63,011)
- September 2020: current status (65,112).

Excellent. The paperwork shows that the mileage rose at a consistent rate of 10,000 per annum. It never fell. In addition, evidence comes from a variety of sources rather, for instance, than only the invoices. That is noteworthy as the seller is unlikely to fake such an enormous range of documentation. Furthermore, there were no long, unsettling periods when the mileage was not recorded. Someone jotted it down every few months.

Note too that the condition of the car is consistent with the claimed mileage. It is not far scruffier than similar vehicles that have comparable mileage. Now consider the invoice items. The car needed new brake discs, new pads, and gas for its air conditioning. It had new tyres and bulbs, too. Fine. It is reasonable to replace these components within the mileage. In contrast, there are not countless invoices for parts that typically last longer than 65,112 miles. The supplying dealership provides further reassurance. It is long established, respected, and popular. For these reasons the mileage is most likely genuine.

Vehicle B

Vehicle B's MOT, service, and invoice history is:

- February 2014: new (0 miles)
- February 2017: MOT 1 (29,282)
- March 2017: service 1 (30,022)
- April 2017: invoice 1, transmission (30,277)
- May 2017: invoice 2, head gasket (32,422)
- February 2018: MOT 2 (39,828)
- March 2018: service 2 (40,632)
- February 2019: MOT 3 (49,223)
- March 2019: service 3 (50,987)
- February 2020: MOT 4 (59,222)
- March 2020: service 4 (60,001)
- September 2020: current status (70,001).

Not good. There are no records for the first 3 years. How likely is it that the keeper failed to maintain the car during this period? It was, after all, at its most valuable and possibly covered by a manufacturer service plan. It is helpful to lose such records if the vehicle is clocked. Furthermore, invoice 1 shows that the transmission broke at 30,277 miles (April 2017). In addition, invoice 2 confirms that the head gasket failed the following month. Odd. Such issues tend to occur at higher mileage.

Furthermore, the condition of the vehicle is below average for 70,001 miles. The seats look far too worn, for example. Such things suggest it was clocked in its first 3 years. Even if the mileage is correct, there is not enough paperwork for the early part of the car's life to buy with confidence. Vehicle B is risky.

Vehicle C

Vehicle C's MOT, service, and invoice history is:

- March 2014: new (0 miles)
- March 2015: service 1 (10,122)
- March 2016: service 2 (20,221)
- October 2016: invoice 1, tyres (25,322)
- March 2017: MOT 1 (39,444)
- April 2017: service 3 (39,933)
- October 2017: invoice 2, battery (28,911)
- March 2018: MOT 2 (35,211)
- April 2018: service 4 (37,358)
- March 2019: MOT 3 (46,249)
- November 2019: invoice 3, tyres (55,111)
- December 2019: invoice 4, exhaust (56,982)
- March 2020: MOT 4 (60,233)
- April 2020: service 5 (61,022)
- September 2020: current status (68,000).

Vehicle C's problem is immediately obvious. From March 2014 to April 2017, the mileage rose from 0 to 39,933. That is fine. However, the mileage then fell. Consider invoice 2 in October 2017, for instance. The mileage was 28,911 which is fewer than the earlier dates. Vehicle C is clocked.

Vehicle D

Vehicle D's MOT, service, and invoice history is:

- October 2017: new (0 miles)
- September 2020: current status (20,126).

Note there is no paperwork whatsoever. There is no service booklet, no invoices, and the vehicle is too young for its first MOT. Not good. How can you have any confidence the mileage is correct? The only evidence is the condition of the vehicle and that alone is insufficient. Whereas there is no proof it is clocked, there is also nothing to suggest otherwise.

Check List 3: Paperwork

Factor 7: Manufacturer Recalls

Consider the Supporting Material that follows, then list any recall issues.

Check List 3: Paperwork

Factor 7: Manufacturer Recalls

Supporting Material

The manufacturer recalls the car – and every other example of its type – if it becomes known there is a major design flaw and/or material defect. Maybe there is a problem with the brakes, for example. The issue is then fixed for free even years after production. This is common and not a reason to panic. In the United Kingdom, there is an online database that lists such issues. Find it via your phone. If there is a recall, look for written proof the work has been completed or ask the manufacturer. Naturally, address any outstanding recalls if you purchase.

Check List 3: Paperwork

Conclusion

Check List 3 is complete so pat yourself on the back. Now review any comments you wrote above and decide whether you want to evaluate the vehicle further. Go home, for instance, if you discovered a serious problem or too many minor issues. In contrast, if the paperwork is acceptable continue to Check List 4.

Check List 4:

Vehicle Inspection

Check List 4: Vehicle Inspection

Contents

Check List 4 helps you evaluate the car in the flesh. For each step consider whether it is necessary, preferable, or safer for it to be switched on or off. Power is not required to check the paint, for example. In contrast, not having power might stop some features working and wrongly suggest they are broken. Naturally, skip any checks for features not fitted to the car and have sensible expectations relative to its age, mileage, and price.

Recognise too that what follows is a comprehensive guide and it might be impractical to complete every step. Perhaps time is against you. Perhaps there is too much traffic. Perhaps the weather is terrible. In such circumstances, it is best to prioritise the checks that are most important to you.

Finally, remember that the car belongs to the seller at this point so you cannot check anything without permission. Permission is implicitly granted for common, predictable tasks such as checking the paint. Such a task is not invasive or alarming. The same might not be said throughout. Perhaps you want to see the spare wheel in the boot but it is hidden under carpet. The seller might be irritated if you remove the carpet without discussion. Ask for additional permission as needed so that you stay on good terms. Check List 4 includes:

- Factor 1: Bodywork
- Factor 2: Doors, Tailgate, Bonnet, and Locks
- Factor 3: Windows
- Factor 4: Mirrors
- Factor 5: Wheels
- Factor 6: Tyres
- Factor 7: Lights

Check List 4: Vehicle Inspection

Factor 1: Bodywork

Consider the Supporting Material that follows, then inspect the bodywork and list any issues.

Check List 4: Vehicle Inspection

Factor 1: Bodywork

Supporting Material

Panel Joints

As the name suggests, a panel joint is a place on the car that adjacent panels meet. Expect a narrow gap or for the panels to touch. When the car left the factory its joints were perfect throughout. They were the shape and size intended by the manufacturer. Are they now? If not, something caused the imperfection. Maybe the car crashed. Maybe it was vandalised.

The joint between the front, right wing and bonnet is a sensible place to start the inspection. Consider first how it looks at its front, centre, and rear. Is it wide? Is it narrow? Do the panels touch? Now compare it to the equivalent joint on the other side of the car. Does it match? Furthermore, the wing and bonnet probably flowed smoothly into each other when the vehicle was new – so note any elevation. If, for instance, part of the wing is now proud it might be bent. It is often easier to feel for elevation with your fingertips than to see it. Go from panel joint to panel joint to repeat your checks.

Rust

A minor rust patch makes the car look scruffy but is not structural, widespread, or obvious from a distance. Perhaps a stone hit the front of the bonnet and broke the paint. Maybe water then attacked the metal and a little rust formed. Whereas it is tempting to ignore such issues, think carefully as rust spreads fast. Even the largest hole started life as a minor blemish. Minor rust has to be fixed before it becomes major.

Major rust is more concerning. It is structural and/or

cosmetically significant. Furthermore, if the vehicle has extremely rusty bodywork it is likely to be in a similar mess elsewhere. That is worrying as rust near certain mechanical parts can be dangerous. The suspension mounts spring to mind. I recently saw a car that had terrible bodywork and this was indicative of serious, widespread, structural flaws. In addition, the fuel pipe was so rusty it leaked so the car was a fire hazard.

Pick a metal panel to evaluate first. A metal panel rather than plastic can be recognised by the noise as you tap it. Expect a heavier tone. Look now for brown blemishes, bubbling paint, and holes. Once complete, move from panel to panel and repeat the checks throughout. Recognise too that some panels suffer more than others. This is because they more often get hit by stones or covered by mud. Pay particular attention to the wheel arches, the lower parts of the doors, and the front of the bonnet.

Dents

A dent looks unsightly so has to be identified on that basis alone. It might also be indicative of further damage. Perhaps there is a dent in the rear bumper. Did the impact also break the exhaust that is in close proximity. Choose a panel to evaluate first, then. A big dent is easy to spot but a smaller mark can be missed. On this basis, improve the odds by viewing the panel low at 90 degrees. For example, to check the driver's door crouch close to the front wing then look towards the rear of the car. Recognise too that water and dirt can conceal blemishes so clean the panel with a soft cloth if necessary. Best not be too vigorous as dirt can scuff the paintwork. Finally, go panel to panel and repeat these checks.

Paint

Consider whether the car has its original paint throughout. If not, it was likely damaged and resprayed. Note too that it is important to only compare metal panels to metal and plastic to plastic. Paint sometimes fades faster on plastic. So, pick a panel and evaluate its paint. When new, it matched every other such panel on the vehicle. Is it now shinier? Is it more vibrant? Also lift any rubber seal. Is the paint beneath different to the more visible parts of the panel? Further signs of respray include:

- paint on the weather seals, trim, and/or badges
- lines where new paint meets old
- drips
- ripples
- orange peel finish.

Now walk around the car again and look for scratches, i.e. lines, swirls, and scuffs. Polish removes or improves slight imperfections but a respray is required to fix deep wounds. Finally, rub your fingertips over the paint. Does it feel very, very smooth? If so, it might be waxed which implies somebody cared for the car. Good. This care might be replicated throughout.

Plastic and Fibreglass Body Panels

There are further specific checks for plastic and fibreglass panels. Choose one then look for cracks, splits, and holes where the material is missing. Now move from panel to panel and repeat.

Cut and Shut

If the vehicle is a cut and shut it is dangerous and must be scrapped immediately. Why? Because its front is the remnants of a car that had a rear impact. In contrast, its rear is what is left of a vehicle that was hit at the front. It is therefore a couple of cars welded together. Many of the aforementioned checks reveal this work. Bad panel joints and new paint, for example. However, also note any peculiar welds. Can you see any on the pillars by the rear window or windscreen, for example? Also check the metal sills that run beneath the doors.

Note too that suspicious welds can be hidden. For instance, those on the pillars might be close to legitimate, original bends on the bodywork. If there is cause for concern, consider whether the vehicle matches other theoretically identical examples. Photographs on the internet might provide confirmation. Furthermore, welds on the underside can be hidden by mechanical components and/or rust prevention treatment. The latter might be sprayed on (or painted). Walk away if you have any suspicion the car is a cut and shut.

Check List 4: Vehicle Inspection

Factor 2: Doors, Tailgate, Bonnet, and Locks

Consider the Supporting Material that follows then check the doors, tailgate, bonnet, and locks and list any faults.

Check List 4: Vehicle Inspection

Factor 2: Doors, Tailgate, Bonnet, and Locks

Supporting Material

Doors

Check the driver's door first. Ensure initially that it is unlocked then pull the exterior handle. Does the door open? If not, perhaps the catch assembly is broken. Consider too whether the door remains open. There is a component called the stay that stops it closing and crushing your leg. Best shut the door too. Does it close properly and sit flush with the adjacent bodywork? Now get in the vehicle, close the door, and check the interior handle works so you can get back out. It is annoying when you cannot. Trust me. I know. Can you guess what once broke on my car?

Consider too whether the door makes a tortured screaming noise as it moves. If so, the probable solution is to lubricate the hinges. That is not a problem. It is a fast, cheap job and among the most basic maintenance tasks. Might a lack of lubrication therefore be indicative of widespread neglect? Go from door to door and repeat these checks.

Soft Close Door System

This system eliminates any need to slam the doors shut. It is useful at night if you want to be quiet. To test it, push the driver's door until it is virtually flush with the adjacent bodywork. Now watch, wait a moment, and ensure it is automatically pulled closed. Move throughout the vehicle and repeat the process.

Tailgate

Open the tailgate to check its catch releases. Does it now rise to its highest position without issue? Does it stay there? If it struggles or feels too heavy the support struts might be weaker than the world's worst larger. Ensure also that the tailgate closes securely. Finally, search the cabin for a lever or button that releases the tailgate remotely. Does it work nicely?

Powered Tailgate

See Tailgate for the test procedure. However, operate it electrically rather than by hand. Further expect an extra button at the rear of the car to shut the tailgate. Does the button work?

Powered Tailgate Limiter

The limiter stops the tailgate rising beyond a height of your choice. It is useful if your garage has a very low roof, for instance. To check it works, note how high the tailgate rises without any restriction. It is as high as the hinges permit. Now set the limiter far lower to provide meaningful contrast. You might have to read the car's manual to learn how. Finally close the tailgate, reopen, then ensure it stops at the specified point.

Kick Tailgate

The kick tailgate opens via motion gesture which is helpful if your arms are full of shopping. To test it, ensure that the vehicle's key fob is in close proximity, wave your foot beneath the centre of the rear bumper, and confirm the tailgate rises.

Bonnet

My friend once spent hours hacking at the front of his vehicle with increasingly vicious tools. Why? Because the bonnet release mechanism failed so he could not access the engine bay. His attempts to rectify the problem broke the grille, cracked the bumper, and left him needing months of therapy.

So, best assess the bonnet of your potential purchase. Simply:

- pull the release lever in the cabin
- ensure the bonnet lifts slightly (listen for a clunk)
- pull the secondary release lever at the front of the car
- open the bonnet.

Note too that something has to hold the bonnet open. Gas struts, for instance. If fitted, ensure the bonnet rises to its highest position with minimal effort from you. Further confirm that it is secure. If not, it might fall so mind your head. Alternatively, the bonnet might be held by an arm you position by hand. Ensure it is present, in good condition, and able to perform its task. Now close the bonnet and check it is secure.

Active Bonnet

The active bonnet is a safety feature. If a pedestrian hits the front of the car its bonnet lifts slightly via a spring. It then bounces to cushion the impact and minimise injury. Clearly, this system cannot be tested on the forecourt. Best look for a warning message on the dashboard that suggests there is a fault.

Manual Locking System

This system requires you to operate the locks individually. Evaluate the key first. Is it straight? A bend might stop it working. Now move to the exterior of the driver's door, lock it, and pull the handle. Is it secure? Can, in contrast, you now unlock the door and open it? Furthermore, note the condition of the lock and its surroundings. Is the key slot wrecked? Is the adjacent metal damaged? If so, perhaps someone forced the door open. Did he/she then take the car for a joy ride and damage it further? Also check the lock works via its inner control. Finally, walk around the car and repeat the checks as appropriate.

Central Locking System

This feature lets you operate the locks simultaneously via a traditional key. To test it, lock the vehicle from the driver's door, circumnavigate its exterior, and check every lock is secure. Pull the handles, in other words. If, for example, the left rear door opens there is a fault. Now return to the driver's door, unlock it, and walk around the car again. Confirm every lock is now open. Get in the car too. Can you see the internal button that operates all the locks simultaneously? Best ensure it works properly. Furthermore, check the key slot and its surroundings for damage indicative of theft. Evaluate the key too. Is it straight?

Remote Central Locking System

See Central Locking System for the test procedure, but use the wireless key fob rather than a key. Furthermore, recognise that the fob is expensive, electronically linked to the car, and that it hangs on a keyring where it can be easily damaged. On this basis, confirm that the fob works properly – not just that it works.

Best consider its range first. A couple of metres is acceptable but far, far further is preferable. If the range is poor the battery is weak or there is a fault. Consider each button too. Do, for example, you have to press lock several times before it reacts? Note too that the fob might have quirks that can be misinterpreted as faults. Maybe only the driver's door opens if you press unlock. A second click might be required to open the other doors. This is more likely to be a configurable option or characteristic than a fault. Check the manual for confirmation.

Keyless Entry System

Keyless entry eliminates any need to interact with the vehicle's key fob to operate its locks. To test it, ensure the fob is in close proximity then pull the driver's door handle. Alternatively, first press a button on the handle then pull it.

Either way, confirm the door opens. Now close it and tap the button. Is the door now locked? Any clunking noise suggests it is. Alternatively:

- press the button
- walk some distance from the vehicle
- abandon the key fob
- go back to the vehicle
- ensure you cannot open the doors.

Automatic Locking System

This system locks the doors and tailgate once the car hits a specified speed. 8 miles per hour, for example. To test it, accelerate slowly and listen for a clunk as the locks engage. However, note that the system might only lock the exterior handles. Its purpose is to lock people out not to lock you inside.

Manual Child Lock System

This feature locks the rear inner door handles so kids cannot let themselves out. However, it has no impact on the exterior handles. Note too that each door has to be configured individually. To start the test, open the right door and find the control on its inner edge. Set the lock via a lever or key. Now open the window, close the door, and lean through the window to check the inner handle is locked. Also pull the exterior handle to check it works normally. Repeat this test opposite.

Electric Child Lock System

See Manual Child Lock System. In contrast, the electric version curtails both inner rear handles via a button by the driver's seat. To test it, open the rear windows and engage the system via the button. Now reach through the rear, right window and ensure the inner handle is locked. Ensure, in contrast, that the outer handle behaves normally. Repeat these checks opposite.

Check List 4: Vehicle Inspection

Factor 3: Windows

Consider the Supporting Material that follows, then check the vehicle's windows and list any problems.

Check List 4: Vehicle Inspection

Factor 3: Windows

Supporting Material

Windscreen

In the United Kingdom the windscreen is split into zones. Zone A is 290 millimetres wide from the centre of the steering wheel. It also extends up and down in the area swept by the windscreen wipers. Expect the vehicle to fail its MOT (annual inspection) if there is an applicable fault that measures 10 millimetres or greater. A stone chip, for example. Zone B is any other area swept by the wipers. Here, any fault 40 millimetres or greater is a problem.

Look first for chips and cracks within the zones. Is there anything bad enough to make the car fail its MOT? Note smaller chips and cracks, too. Bouncing down the road might make them spread. Also check for serious scratches that impede visibility. Look for problems outside the zones, too. Furthermore, recognise that the windscreen incorporates multiple layers as it is not a single piece of glass. Are the layers properly stuck together or separating? A milky look suggests separation.

Side Windows

Start the inspection at the driver's window. The first step is to confirm it is present. It is easy to assume that a missing window is merely an open window. That is a costly mistake. Ensure the glass is glass, too. Perspex is a cheap replacement if the original is broken. Now check for chips, cracks, and scratches that make it hard to see through. Repeat the checks for the other side windows.

Rear Window

See Side Windows if the window is made of glass. In contrast, if the car is a convertible it might have a flexible, plastic, rear window to help the roof open. The potential problems include:

- discolouration
- permanently foggy
- splits
- not sealed properly to the roof.

Privacy Glass

Consider whether the car has after market privacy glass, i.e. a layer of tinted film added since it left the factory. In the United Kingdom, the windscreen must let 75 percent of the exterior light penetrate the cabin if the vehicle was registered from April 1985. The front side windows must let 70 percent through. These figures include any tint permanently integrated at manufacturer plus any additional, after market film. There are no such restrictions for the windows further back.

First check the interior of the windscreen for film. Bubbles, creases, and/or a lip around its edge make it easy to see. Now move throughout the car to repeat. If you see film, the challenge is to prove it is legal. A light sensor provides peace of mind but I doubt you own one. Alternatively, maybe you saw a related invoice among the paperwork for Check List 3. Does it say how much tint was added? If not, it might at least confirm it was fitted by a professional who knew the law. More worrying is if it was fitted by the keeper. Either way, film can be peeled off easily so it is not a reason to abandon the vehicle.

Manual Window System

Start at the driver's window and confirm the handle is present, secure, and intact. Cracks suggest it is on borrowed time. Check the mechanism too. Does the handle turn without excess force? Does the window open? Does it close? Repeat the checks throughout the car. However, recognise that it is not necessarily a fault if a rear window cannot lower completely into its door. It is more likely a characteristic. If required, cross reference with the window opposite for peace of mind.

Front Electric Window System

Find the master panel by the driver's seat that controls both front windows. Now open the driver's window. Does it lower without stopping, taking too long, or reversing course? Now close the window and apply the same criteria. Furthermore, find the switch on the master panel for the front passenger window, and repeat. Perhaps these steps confirm that both windows work via the master panel. You might therefore assume all is well throughout. That is risky. I recently saw a passenger window open via the master panel but not from the secondary switch the passenger relies on. Test the secondary switch, then. Finally, go to the back of the car and evaluate any manual windows. See Manual Window System for insight.

Front and Rear Electric Window System

See Front Electric Window System but expand the procedure to include the rear windows.

Electric Window Safety System

This system stops the windows closing if they are likely to trap your fingers. To test it, open the driver's window and block its path back to the top with something that cannot hurt the car. A newspaper is ideal. Now start to close the window but ensure it stops as it senses the hazard. Move throughout the car and repeat.

Electric Window Lock System

This feature locks the rear windows and possibly the front passenger window. Its purpose is to stop children lowering the glass. To test it, engage the system then go from window to window to check the switches are locked. However, you can probably still operate all the windows from your master panel.

Heated Windscreen

The heated windscreen removes frost and condensation via very thin, barely visible, heated wires within. If, by chance, the windscreen requires such attention switch the system on, wait a while, and confirm it starts to clear. Ensure there is no help from the vehicle's interior fans. In contrast, if there is no frost or condensation touch the windscreen to check it feels warm.

Rear Window Demist

See Heated Windscreen but test the back window.

Manual Sunroof

The sunroof is a window above the front seats that likely has a dark, factory tint. Look first for cracks and chips. They might let water into the cabin. You then take an involuntary shower if it rains. Furthermore, check the rubber seal that surrounds the sunroof. Is it complete? Is it split? Is it too dry? Is there anything that implies it leaks such as stains on the roof lining? Ensure too that the sunroof completes its full range of movement without issue. So, are the controls present and in good condition? Does the sunroof lift slightly at its rear edge? Does it slide out of sight within the roof? Does it close properly? I once had a sunroof jam open during a long motorway journey. At least the rain stopped me getting dehydrated.

Furthermore, the sunroof has drainage channels that let water escape the confines of the vehicle. This is far preferable than letting it pool. The entry holes to these channels might be visible so look for blockages. The probable location is below where the front corners of the sunroof sit once it is shut. Best open the sunroof and have a look. If there is a blockage, the likely solution is to clear it with a toothpick or compressed air.

There might also be a blind below the sunroof on the interior of the car. As needed, its purpose is to block the sun so it cannot boil your head. Confirm the blind moves forward and backward.

Electric Sunroof

See Manual Sunroof for the test procedure. However, rather than move the glass manually ensure the electric motor and switches operate properly. Does the sunroof complete its full range of movement without struggling, stopping, or taking too long?

Panoramic Roof

The panoramic roof is best perceived as a very large sunroof. See Manual Sunroof and Electric Sunroof for the test suggestions.

Check List 4: Vehicle Inspection

Factor 4: Mirrors

Consider the Supporting Material that follows, then inspect the mirrors and list any faults.

Check List 4: Vehicle Inspection

Factor 4: Mirrors

Supporting Material

The car has external and internal mirrors. Ensure each is:

- present
- intact, e.g. not chipped or cracked
- secure in its housing
- good quality, i.e. not a blurry after market replacement.

In addition, some mirrors have features that make them more than simple reflective surfaces. Best consider the advanced checks below.

Manual Door Mirror Adjustment System

The system incorporates a small wand in the cabin for each exterior mirror. They move the mirrors to the appropriate positions. To test the system, find the wand for the mirror nearest the driver's seat. It is probably on the pillar by the windscreen. Now ensure the wand is in good condition so not likely to snap in the near future. Confirm too that the mirror moves a significant distance in every direction. Does it move far enough left, for example? Repeat these steps for the other mirror.

Electric Door Mirror Adjustment System

This feature enables you to adjust the exterior mirrors electrically. To test it, find the buttons then evaluate the mirror to your right. Does it move an appropriate distance in every direction? Repeat opposite. Furthermore, as you select reverse gear the mirrors might drop to provide a better view of the lines as you reverse into a parking bay. If so, ensure they return to their former positions as you move into first gear. In contrast, it is possible only a single mirror behaves in this fashion. Confirmation comes from the car's manual or the internet.

Manual Fold Door Mirror System

While parked, this system lets you fold the mirrors flatter against the sides of the car to reduce its width. There is then less chance of being hit by any traffic. Start your test at the mirror by the driver's seat. How? Push it towards the side window and check it folds. This might require more force than is comfortable but best not be too rough. Might it be sensible to play safe and ask the seller to fold it? Confirm the mirror also slides back to its former position. Repeat the procedure opposite.

Electric Fold Door Mirror System

See Manual Fold Door Mirror System. However, move the mirrors electrically via a button in the cabin or on the fob. Ensure both:

- operate in unison
- move in the same direction
- stop against the side of the vehicle
- return to their former positions once instructed.

If the movement is inconsistent the system might have to be synchronised. This is not likely to be too troublesome. In contrast, if only the left or right mirror moves there might be a more serious issue opposite. Perhaps the motor is broken.

Heated Exterior Mirror System

This feature removes frost and condensation from the exterior mirrors to improve visibility. To test it, switch on and ensure both mirrors start to clear. But what if there is no frost or condensation? In this scenario, first touch the mirror on the right of the vehicle with your fingertips. Note how it feels. Cool, perhaps. Now switch the system on and wait. Is the glass now warmer? Expect a soft heat rather than a furnace. Repeat opposite.

Manual Rear-view Mirror

This mirror sits in the centre of the windscreen at the top. Ensure first that it moves a significant distance in every direction. Far enough to the left, for example. Furthermore, look for a lever at its base. Its purpose is to point the mirror slightly towards the roof. Less of the dazzling light from the following car is then reflected at your eyes. Does the lever work?

Electric Rear-view Mirror

See Manual Rear-view Mirror. In contrast, move it to position via a motor rather than by hand. Does the motor work? Does the mirror move a suitable distance in every direction?

Dimming Rear-view Mirror

The mirror darkens when it might otherwise reflect dazzling light from the following car at your eyes. To test it, note that the mirror might be permanently on or have to be activated via a button. Activate it if required. Now shine a torch at the light sensor, then ensure the mirror gets significantly darker within seconds. Does the mirror get lighter once you turn off the torch?

Vanity Mirrors

A vanity mirror lives within your sun visor and lets you check your appearance. Never fear! You look amazing! Lower the visor to reveal the mirror and start your inspection. Is the mirror intact? Is it reasonable quality? Does its protective cover open and close? Repeat the test for the mirror opposite.

Check List 4: Vehicle Inspection

Factor 5: Wheels

Consider the Supporting Material that follows, then list any concerns that relate to the wheels.

Check List 4: Vehicle Inspection

Factor 5: Wheels

Supporting Material

Alloy Wheel Set

The alloy wheel set incorporates a smart, high quality finish. Start the inspection at the front, right wheel and check for cracks and dents. These dangerous faults can be caused by hitting a pothole. Less troublesome are cosmetic blemishes such as kerb scuffs and flaking paint. Note corrosion too. It looks bad, but more importantly it might stop the tyre sealing properly. The consequence is that it constantly loses air. What a hassle! Finally, go from wheel to wheel and repeat your checks. Remember the spare.

Steel Wheel Set

A steel wheel set has a less glamorous look than its alloy counterpart. Each wheel therefore has a hubcap to make it look smart. Pick a wheel and check its cap. Is it present? Is it in good condition? Look for cracks, chips, and scuffs. Also, note whether the pattern matches the other caps. If not, it is from a different set. Best not worry too much if the hubcap looks terrible. You can purchase a new set for a modest price.

Furthermore, recognise that the hubcap is pushed onto the wheel rather than secured by nuts and bolts. At best it is further attached by cable ties. It can therefore be removed easily with the seller's permission. In this scenario, check the wheel for cracks and dents that make it dangerous. Note corrosion and kerb marks too. Finally, go wheel to wheel and repeat.

Wheel Nuts

Start the inspection at the front right wheel. Check first that every nut is present. Also confirm the heads are in decent condition. If not, it might be hard to fit the spare tyre if you get a puncture at the roadside. Finally, go wheel to wheel and repeat your checks. If you cannot immediately see the nuts either:

- take off the hubcap if the car has steel wheels
- detach a single piece of trim that covers all the nuts
- remove a plastic cap from each nut.

Locking Wheel Nut System

This system stops the wheels being removed without an adaptor, so it deters theft. Start the inspection at the front, right wheel. Can you see a single locking nut? The odd shape makes it easy to spot. Now go wheel to wheel and repeat. Also, find the adaptor that undoes the nuts. It is a small item that looks like part of a socket set. Consider where it is likely stored. Mine is under the carpet in the boot in a designated hole.

Check List 4: Vehicle Inspection

Factor 6: Tyres

Consider the Supporting Material that follows, then check the tyres and list any defects.

....
....
....
....
....
....
....
....
....
....
....
....
....
....
....
....
....
....
....
....
....
....
....
....
....
....
....
....
....
....
....

Check List 4: Vehicle Inspection

Factor 6: Tyres

Supporting Material

Tyres influence how the vehicle brakes, accelerates, and handles so it is important to check them carefully. Start the inspection at the front, right tyre and note its tread depth. In the United Kingdom, the legal minimum is 1.6 millimetres for the central 75 percent of the tyre's width and around its circumference. You can measure via a gauge. Alternatively, check the numerous wear markers which are small, rectangular pieces of rubber. If the tyre is new, these markers sit deep within the tread pattern. At the bottom of the grooves, in other words. Once the tyre is at – or below – the legal limit the wear markers sit flush with the rest of the tread.

There is more to consider. Look now for bulges in the sidewall that prove the tyre has a major structural flaw. Check too for cracks, tears, and foreign objects such as nails. Also note the stamp on the sidewall that proves when the tyre was made. 51 20, for example. The 51 reveals the week of the year, i.e. 51 of 52. The 20 confirms the year, i.e. 2020. Be cautious if the tyre is old. Performance diminishes with age even if it looks new. Constant exposure to weather takes a toll. What age to replace the tyre is subjective but there is a trusted, long established supplier that says 7 to 10 years. Another says 5.

Consider the brand too. Naturally, it is preferable to have a premium quality tyre than a budget counterpart. Goodyear, Bridgestone, and Michelin are among the brands that tend to impress. Furthermore, inspect the code on the sidewall that defines the specification of the tyre. 215/50 R17 91 V, perhaps. The 215 confirms its width in millimetres. The 50 is the height of the sidewall as a percentage of the width. Also:

- R proves the tyre has a radial construction
- 17 confirms it fits a 17” wheel
- 91 is the load rating (how much weight it can carry)
- V is the speed rating (maximum permitted speed).

On this basis, confirm the tyre meets the manufacturer’s recommendations. Is it the correct size? Does it support enough weight? Confirmation might come via the car’s manual, a sticker on its door pillar, or a sticker in the fuel flap. Naturally, go from tyre to tyre and repeat these checks. Finally, consider whether the make and model of tyre match throughout. Mismatched tyres can impede performance. That said, although unusual it is possible the vehicle’s manufacturer fitted different size tyres at the front and rear.

Puncture Repair Kit

The repair kit is the smaller, lighter alternative to a spare tyre. It contains an electric pump and a can of sealant. The pump forces sealant into the tyre to fill the hole. Check the kit is complete to start the test. Now connect the pump to the car’s power socket, switch it on, and point the nozzle at your hand. Does air emerge at a fair pressure? Ensure too that the can is full rather than leftover from a past repair. Does it feel empty?

Tyre Pressure Monitor System

This system monitors the tyre pressures then reports any problems. To test it, check via a gauge that every tyre has the correct pressure. Now ensure there is no warning message to the contrary. In addition, lower the pressure at the front, right tyre and check a warning appears on the dashboard. If relevant, ensure too that it says which tyre needs attention. Now reinflate the tyre and go wheel to wheel to repeat the process. In contrast, the system might not trigger a warning message until the vehicle moves. That is a pain as it is unwise to drive with poorly inflated tyres. Your safety is compromised.

Check List 4: Vehicle Inspection

Factor 7: Lights

Consider the Supporting Material that follows, then evaluate the lights and jot down any concerns.

Check List 4: Vehicle Inspection

Factor 7: Lights

Supporting Material

Halogen, Xenon, and Bi-xenon Headlamps

Start the inspection at the lamp on the right. Is it chipped, cracked, or smashed? Now check it has a clear, transparent look rather than opaque. If the latter, it resembles a glass that spent too long in the dishwasher. That impedes visibility. Now look through the lens. Can you see a lot of pooled water? If so, there is probably a leak even if there is no obvious damage. Less troubling is a little condensation. This is common, not necessarily a fault, and likely to clear without intervention.

Furthermore, note that the headlamp incorporates a range of lights. Check then that the parking light, headlight, and main beam come on as required. Also ensure they shine brightly and consistently. No flickering, please. These steps prove the bulbs work which is important. Replacements can be very expensive. You might need a mortgage. Equally, the tests confirm that the switches, the headlamp itself, and any parts in between meet expectation. You might learn other things, too. If, for example, the lights flicker maybe the alternator is failing. Its job is to charge the battery that helps start the engine.

Move now to the headlamp on the left of the car and repeat the checks. Consider consistency, too. Perhaps the left lamp looks old, opaque, and weathered yet its counterpart looks new. The likely explanation is that the right headlamp is a replacement. Perhaps its predecessor was broken by a stone. That is of little concern now. However, maybe it was wrecked when the car crashed. Have you seen any further signs of collision damage?

Other Exterior Lights

Naturally, there are other exterior lights. Many of the aforementioned checks apply so walk around the car and repeat as appropriate. However, note that some lights only operate in certain conditions. You probably have to switch on the headlights before the fog lights work, for instance. Also, it is easier to test lights with help from a friend. For example, you cannot press the brake pedal and simultaneously stand behind the car. If you cannot find help, reverse towards a window then look for reflections. Possible lights to test include:

- brake (rear right, rear left, rear centre)
- indicators (rear right, rear left, front right, front left, side right, side left)
- registration plate (rear right, rear left, rear centre)
- tail (rear right, rear left)
- daytime running (front right, front left)
- fog (front right, front left, rear)
- door mirror puddle lights (side right, side left).

Automatic Headlight System

This system automatically switches the lights on and off as required. On this basis, it is easy to conclude it has to be tested at night. This is not necessarily true. See if you can locate the light sensor. It is probably close to the rear-view mirror or on the dashboard. Now cover the light sensor with your hand. This makes the system think it is dark. Do the headlights come on? Now move your hand. Do the headlights go off?

Smart High Beam System

This feature switches between the main beams and standard headlights as required (automatically). Its purpose is to optimise your view and stop you dazzling other drivers. To test it, find a dark road that has patchy, intermittent traffic and stay far back from any vehicles ahead on your side of the road. If detected, these vehicles might stop the system engaging the more powerful lights. Now activate the system and ensure the main beams are on. Furthermore, as a car comes toward you check they go off and the headlights stay lit. Ensure the main beams come back on once the car passes.

Manual Headlamp Leveller System

The manual leveller lets you simultaneously point the headlamps higher or lower. Why bother? Because perhaps they point so high that your view is impeded. Perhaps they also dazzle other motorists. To confirm the system works:

- point the front of the car at a flat surface
- switch on the headlights
- note where the light from the left lamp lands
- ensure you can move it up and down
- repeat these steps for the headlamp opposite.

Automatic Headlamp Leveller System

See Manual Headlamp Leveller System for insight. In contrast, the system works autonomously so it is harder to test on the forecourt. There is hope, though. Point the vehicle at a wall and turn on the headlights. Does the light from the left headlamp strike the surface low then rise to its optimum position? Repeat this process for the headlamp on the opposite side of the car. Although not guaranteed, such movement implies that your automatic levelling system works.

Follow Me Home Light System

Once the car has been parked and switched off, this system ensures some of its exterior lights stay lit. Why? To illuminate the route to your front door so there is less chance of falling. To test it:

- ensure the system is on
- switch the vehicle off
- get out
- lock the doors
- check the lights stay lit for a short time, then go off.

Static Cornering Light System

This feature improves visibility as you make low speed turns. Go left, for example, then an additional light comes to life on the relevant side of the car to illuminate the corner. To test it:

- switch the headlights on
- turn the steering wheel left
- get out the vehicle
- check an extra light on the left is lit
- repeat the test in the opposite direction.

Active Corning light System

The active cornering system ensures the headlights turn with the steering to better illuminate the road. To test it, switch the lights on then point the vehicle at a flat surface. A fence is perfect. Note too where the light from the left lamp hits the surface. Now turn the steering left and right. Does the light follow as required? Repeat these steps for the other headlight.

Interior Function Lights

Interior function lights make it easier to read the instrument cluster and dashboard in low light. It might, for example, be tricky to see how much fuel you have left without any illumination. Other lights might reveal what gear is selected, where the heater controls are, and how to turn on the radio. To check all is well, switch on the headlights and ensure the interior lights up as required. Odd dark spots suggest trouble.

Interior Convenience Lights

The vehicle likely has a wide range of interior convenience lights. Ensure each is intact, dry, and working properly. Some might only work if your headlights are switched on. Check any:

- ceiling (front, rear, centre)
- map reading (front left, front right)
- boot light (left, right, centre)
- door puddle (front right, front left, rear right, rear left)
- key slot
- glovebox
- ambient mood.

Final Thought

Ensure that every exterior light works without impeding its bedfellows. Note my experience. I once tested my brake lights and they worked. There was a problem, though. As I braked the reversing light came on, too. This complemented a range of other issues. The rear fog light came on as I indicated left, cruise control went off as I indicated right, and the reversing camera worked in forward gears. The fault was traced to a dirty wire in the rear, left light. It is remarkable what dirt can do to a car.

Check List 4: Vehicle Inspection

Factor 8: Wipers and Washers

Consider the Supporting Material that follows, then check the wipers and washers and list any problems.

Check List 4: Vehicle Inspection

Factor 8: Wipers and Washers

Supporting Material

Wipers

Pick a windscreen wiper and check its rubber blade. Splits and a lack of flexibility confirm it is time to get a replacement. However, even if the blade looks new test it further via the window washing system. Simply fire a lot of water at the windscreen to see how the blade performs. Expect a new, high quality blade to remove the vast majority of the water in a single pass without streaking. Does it? Perhaps make some allowance if the windscreen is very dirty. Finally, if the blade is old and/or bad quality it might squeak and/or vibrate too much.

Consider also how the wiper travels. Confirm it is smoothly, in unison with any counterpart adjacent, and that it sweeps the intended part of the windscreen. Check it does not miss a section to the right, for instance. Ensure the travel is not excessive, though. Warning signs include knocking at either end of the stroke. Maybe in this scenario the wiper has to be adjusted. Perhaps, in contrast, there is a fault or the blade is the wrong size. Repeat these steps for any adjacent and rear wiper. Furthermore, assess any speed and frequency settings.

Automatic Windscreen Wiping System

The automatic wiping system springs to life once a sensor concludes it is raining. To test it, switch on and confirm the wipers move if the screen is wet. Check too that the speed and frequency increase if it rains harder. Ensure, in contrast, that the wipers slow and stop as required. If there is no rain, spray the windscreen with bottled water or splash through a few puddles.

Window Washing System

This system fires water at the windscreen to remove dirt. It incorporates a reservoir, electric pump, and jets. To test it, ensure that water emerges with enough force to hit the screen. No ineffective dribbles, please. If nothing emerges, check whether the reservoir is empty before concluding there is a fault. Perhaps there is a warning message on the dashboard. Confirm too that water fires from every jet. If, for example, only the left jets fire the pipe opposite might be blocked. Repeat your checks for the rear window.

Note: While parked, it is preferable for water to hit the windscreen no higher than half way up. Why? Because air rushes over the screen as you drive and pushes the water higher. On this basis, if it hits the screen too high while parked the air pushes it over the roof as you drive. The jets can be adjusted if needed.

Headlamp Washer System

This system propels water at the headlamps to remove debris. The jets either sit close to the lamps or emerge from the bumper on stalks as required. Either way, they make great water pistols as my partner knows to her cost. Note that there might not be a specific button to engage the system. It might, for example, come to life automatically every fifth clean of the windscreen. The headlights might have to be turned on, too. The test procedure is:

- engage the system
- get out of the car
- ensure both headlamps are wet
- check both stalks are back in the bumper (if relevant).

Check List 4: Vehicle Inspection

Factor 9: Registration Plates & Registration

Consider the Supporting Material that follows, then check the registration plates – and the registration itself – and list any issues.

Check List 4: Vehicle Inspection

Factor 9: Registration Plates & Registration

Supporting Material

It is important to distinguish between the car's registration plates and the registration itself. The plates are the large, plastic, rectangular components that attach to the front and rear. In comparison, the registration is the series of letters and numbers printed on the plates that give the car a unique identity.

Check the rear registration plate first. Is it present? Is it intact? Is it securely attached? Are the characters damaged? Furthermore, the plate cannot be obscured by a tow bar, stickers, or anything else. Anything that makes it tricky to read is a potential problem. Repeat these checks for the plate at the front.

Now consider the registration itself, i.e. the unique series of letters and numbers. Recognise first that it incorporates a specific format assuming it is a standard, non personal type. But what format? Perhaps the vehicle was new from September 2001 in the United Kingdom. If so, the legal format from left to right is:

- 2 letters (confirms where the car was registered)
- 2 numbers (reveals when the car was registered)
- Space (makes the registration easier to read)
- 3 letters (random).

The plates must display this registration format in a specific manner. The characters must be 79mm tall and 14mm thick. Further requirements relate to width, font, and spacing. You get in trouble if the car falls foul. Clearly, it is not sensible, practical, or necessary to measure the characters but take an overview. Note the rear plate first. Now broadly compare it to other plates that have the same format. Maybe there are cars parked across the road. Look for obvious discrepancies such as an odd font. Repeat this process for the plate at the front.

Retention of Registration

Recognise too that the registration is not tied to the car for life. In the United Kingdom, the keeper can therefore sell the vehicle but retain its registration. The latter might then be transferred to another vehicle. Confirm then whether the registration is part of the sale. It is more likely to be retained if it is personal. Naturally, there are implications if the car is separated from its registration. It needs an immediate replacement, for starters. Does the seller expect you to arrange it? Does the seller expect you to pay? Clarify such things.

In contrast, perhaps the car has a personal registration that is part of the sale. Good. It might be valuable. You can therefore buy the vehicle then sell its registration. You might earn a bit of money. However, be careful not to overpay especially if the seller claims the registration is valuable. How do you know this is true? The solution is to have it independently valued by a company that sells registrations. There is a lot of choice online.

Check List 4: Vehicle Inspection

Factor 10: Tow Bar

Consider the Supporting Material that follows, then note any evidence that suggests someone has removed a tow bar.

Check List 4: Vehicle Inspection

Factor 10: Tow Bar

Supporting Material

Check List 2 explained how to evaluate pictures of the vehicle before travelling to see it in person. It confirmed it is important to spot a tow bar, for instance. Towing increases wear and wear equates to cost. On this basis, there is a couple of potential scenarios. The first is that you saw a tow bar but chose to the visit the car anyway. The second is that no bar was visible. If the latter, it is possible someone removed it to conceal the car's past or for less mischievous reasons. Check for:

- tow ball removed but the mount remains
- leftover electrical connections
- cut out in the rear bumper (this is rare)
- vehicle missing its rear crash barrier.

Check List 4: Vehicle Inspection

Factor 11: Badges, Bonnet Ornament, & Trim

Consider the Supporting Material that follows then check the badges, bonnet ornament, and trim and list any issues.

....

....

....

....

....

....

....

....

....

....

....

....

....

....

....

....

....

....

....

....

....

....

....

....

....

....

....

....

....

....

....

Check List 4: Vehicle Inspection

Factor 11: Badges, Bonnet Ornament, & Trim

Supporting Material

Badges

Note any badges on the vehicle. They might prove what engine and trim level it has. Ensure such facts match the paperwork and the advertising. The advert might claim the vehicle is top of the range but its badges might suggest otherwise, for example. Is the seller lying or making an honest mistake? Also ensure the badges are present and in reasonable condition. Replacements might be tricky to source.

Bonnet Ornament

Any large, prominent bonnet ornament is probably an after market addition if the car is fairly modern. It is unlikely the manufacturer fitted it at the factory, in other words. This is because it increases the risk of hurting a pedestrian if there is a collision. Furthermore, to fit the ornament someone drilled holes through the metal bonnet. Oh dear! This removed the finish that prevented rust. Did he/she then replace the finish or leave the metal exposed to bad weather? Is there any rust?

Trim

The vehicle likely has exterior plastic trim. If so, circumnavigate it and ensure each piece is present, securely attached, and in good condition. Look for cracks, scuffs, and discolouration. However, there is little cause for concern if any black trim has faded. There are low cost products that restore the shine.

Check List 4: Vehicle Inspection

Factor 12: Internal Combustion Engine

Consider the Supporting Material that follows, then check the engine and list any concerns.

Check List 4: Vehicle Inspection

Factor 12: Internal Combustion Engine

Supporting Material

A little mechanical knowledge makes it easier to check the engine. Never fear, though. The following explanation is not strenuous. At the core of the engine is its block which is a large, heavy, metal component that contains hollow tubes called cylinders. When referring to the engine, note how many cylinders it has and their relative positions. Perhaps it is a 4-cylinder in-line. If so, it has 4 cylinders that sit vertically in a line. Or is it a V8. If so, it has 8 cylinders arranged like a letter V (4 each side). A flat 6 therefore has 6 cylinders that lie horizontally in the engine bay. There are numerous configurations.

The cylinders have a combined capacity measured in litres. 2.0 litres, for example. The larger the capacity the more potential there is for power. Note potential for power - not power itself. There is no guarantee that a big engine has more power than a smaller counterpart. Other factors play a part. When referring to the engine, add its capacity and fuel type to the terms previously explained. Perhaps it is a 2.0 litre, 4-cylinder, in-line, petrol.

There is more to consider. Perceive the engine block as a metal biscuit tin that contains various goodies. A tin needs a lid. The cylinder head is that lid. Note too that the block and head have to be sealed tightly together. The engine can then withstand the high internal pressure required to produce power. The head gasket provides this seal. It sits between the block and the head. In addition, each cylinder contains a piston which is a metal, tube shaped part that moves up and down. Each cylinder and piston repeatedly run through a cycle.

If the car is modern the cycle is:

- piston starts at the top of the cylinder
- piston moves down
- intake valves in the cylinder head open
- air sucked into the cylinder through the intake valves
- intake valves close
- injector fires fuel into the cylinder
- piston moves up to compress the fuel and air
- mixture ignites (the catalyst is a spark plug if the engine burns petrol or compression if it burns diesel)
- explosion forces the piston down
- piston moves up
- waste material from the combustion process is pushed through the now open exhaust valves.

Furthermore, each piston is attached by a connecting rod to the crankshaft at the bottom of the engine. The purpose of the crankshaft is to convert the reciprocating (up and down) movement of the pistons into rotational motion. Why is beyond the remit of this book. However, note the term revolutions per minute as measured by the tachometer (rev counter) on the dashboard. This figure reveals how many times the crankshaft spins in 60 seconds. It is best perceived as the engine speed. Naturally, do not confuse the engine speed with the velocity of your car as it travels down the road.

Note too that the revolutions per minute are low if the car is waiting at a junction. Typically expect 800 to 1,000 if the engine is warm and healthy. The figure then rises to several thousand if you accelerate hard. Through various nuts, bolts, and electronics the revolutions of the crankshaft are transferred to the wheels. The car can then move. Great stuff!

Engine Oil

Time to start the inspection. Recognise first that the engine craves oil like a shopaholic craves credit cards. Its purpose is to lubricate, clean, and cool key components. Without it, the engine's life expectancy can be measured in minutes. Clearly, it is important to check how much oil the engine contains relative to the manufacturer's recommendation. The process is:

- park on a flat surface
- switch the engine off
- ensure the transmission is in neutral (or park)
- confirm the parking brake is engaged
- wait a few minutes for the oil to settle
- open the bonnet
- find the dipstick which is a long, thin, metal strip that extends deep into the block until only its handle is seen
- remove the dipstick
- wipe off any oil that might distort the reading
- replace the dipstick
- remove the dipstick a second time
- take a reading via the high and low marks
- replace the dipstick.

Maybe the oil level is far too low. At best, this suggests whoever last changed the oil miscalculated which hardly inspires confidence. What other mistakes were made? In contrast, there might be a leak so look for oil in the engine bay, on the underside of the vehicle, and/or pooled on the ground. Alternatively, maybe the level is low because the engine burns a lot of oil. This might be indicative of a problem.

In contrast, perhaps the level is far too high. That too is a serious problem. The excess oil pools at the bottom of the engine then get whipped into a light, airy foam by the spinning crankshaft. The foam makes it hard for the pump to circulate enough good oil to properly cool, clean, and lubricate the engine. Despite being too full it gets starved of oil. How ironic!

Now note the condition of the engine oil on the tip of the dipstick. Expect it to have a transparent, golden brown colour if it is brand new. In contrast, if it is black it contains waste material from the engine's combustion process. This change can take a long time if the car has a healthy, regularly serviced petrol engine but be fast if it has an old diesel. On this basis, black may or may not imply the oil is old. Perhaps its texture provides confirmation. Rub a sample between your fingers and thumb. New oil in a healthy engine is silky smooth.

Head Gasket

As mentioned, the head gasket seals the engine block to the cylinder head. Furthermore the fuel, oil, and coolant that circulate throughout the engine have to be kept separate and the gasket facilitates. But why bother to separate these liquids? Because contaminated oil cannot lubricate effectively and contaminated coolant cannot cool properly. That is bad, bad news. A badly lubricated, badly cooled engine is on borrowed time. So, best check whether your gasket is leaking.

To look for issues, remove the oil filler cap at the top of the engine. Now inspect its underside and the pipe it covers. Can you see a thick creamy substance called mayonnaise? Check the oil on the dipstick, too. Does it look creamy? Mayonnaise forms when water mixes with oil so its presence suggests the gasket leaks. Alternatively, the water comes from condensation which is less of a worry. If the latter, a long run might burn it off. Remember that after the test drive. On this basis, mayonnaise does not prove the gasket leaks but that further investigation is required. Other signs of failure include:

- loss of power (due to a lack of pressure in the engine)
- excessive white smoke from the exhaust (because coolant is leaking into the cylinders then burning)
- blue smoke from the exhaust (because oil is leaking into the cylinders then burning)
- engine overheats (because the coolant is contaminated).

Timing Belt

Among other things, the timing belt controls the movement of the valves in the cylinder head. It helps them open and close at the right moment. The manufacturer says it is best to replace the timing belt after a certain number of years or miles. If instead you wait for it to snap, it might wreck other components. On this basis it is important to know whether the car:

- requires a belt now
- requires a belt soon
- requires a belt far, far, in the future
- required a belt in the past
- has a timing chain rather than a belt that performs the same function (but is more likely to last the life of the car).

There is no single rule that confirms when to replace the timing belt on any car. There is too much variation. It is not even sufficient to say that a particular make and model needs the work at a certain point. Why? Because it might be available with a range of engines that have different requirements. The 2.0 litre petrol might need a replacement belt sooner than the 1.6 litre diesel, for example. Vehicle specific research is therefore required. Talk to the manufacture, check the owner's manual, or look online. Note the:

- make
- model
- generation, e.g. mark 3
- engine, e.g. 2.0 litre 150 brake horsepower
- fuel type, e.g. petrol
- year, e.g. 2019.

Perhaps the manufacturer says replace the timing belt at 80,000 miles or 8 years (whichever is sooner). Naturally, no immediate action is required if the car's mileage is far, far fewer and it is far younger. If, in contrast, the belt is due now or was in the past look for evidence the work has been completed. Perhaps the mechanic wrote 'belt at 81,343' beneath the bonnet. Hopefully any such statement is true rather than a ploy. An invoice provides reassurance. Did you see it as you completed Check List 3? If there is no proof otherwise, assume the work is outstanding and budget accordingly. Make the same allowance if the car needs a belt soon.

Noise

The engine makes noises that suggest whether it is healthy or formulating an evil plan to wreck your day, week, or life. On this basis, it might be fair to assume that I can send you an audio file that reveals the optimum tone. No! It cannot be done. The problem, for example, is that a healthy 5.0 litre V8 sounds different to a 1.0 litre 4-cylinder. It is also tricky to know without practical experience whether a peculiar noise comes from the engine or a secondary system connected to it.

However, there is hope as some noises raise an eyebrow whatever the engine. For instance, as mentioned, a piston is attached to the crankshaft lower in the block via a connecting rod. A knocking implies that the rod's bearing is worn. In contrast, a bell tone suggests the piston is lose in its cylinder. Note any clicking too. It implies there is an issue with the valves. Naturally, these noises can be caused by other issues.

Listen for noises when the engine is cold, hot, at high revolutions, and low. Listen too while the car is stationary and throughout the test drive. If necessary, watch videos online in which other drivers demonstrate the type of noises it is important to note. Hope for a smooth, effortless, healthy purr that is free from the aforementioned gremlins. Further listen for:

- splutters
- erratic speed variations
- likely to cut out (or cuts out).

Vibration

The engine has countless parts that move at high speed so expect vibration. Ensure it is not excessive, though. To check for issues, open the bonnet and ask a friend to start the engine. Now watch. If it leaps around like a possessed tumble dryer there might be a problem. Any issue might be exaggerated if your friend presses the throttle. Furthermore, put your hand on the engine if there is a safe position. Be very, very careful though. Pick a spot that is cool and far from any moving parts that might remove your fingers. Now note whether there is too much vibration. Naturally, it is tricky to define how much is too much. Best inspect a few engines to you have points of comparison. Compare it to your current car, for instance. Possible causes of excess vibration include:

- worn engine mounts
- faulty spark plugs
- dodgy timing belt

- internal damage
- fuel delivery problems
- earthquake.

Auxiliary Drive Belt

The auxiliary drive belt is a long, narrow, rubber strip that transfers power from the engine to secondary systems. The alternator, for example. It therefore spins at high speed so mileage takes its toll. To test it, start the engine and listen for squealing that implies the belt slips on its pulley. Now switch the engine off, open the bonnet, and find the belt. Note that it has a smooth front, a grooved rear, and that it can be twisted slightly to optimise your view. Now look for problems such as:

- cracks
- tears
- frays
- missing bits.

Check Engine Light

This light on the dashboard confirms whether the vehicle thinks its engine is faulty. On this basis, start it and check the light comes on. Now ensure it vanishes seconds later. If it stays lit it is indicating a fault. But what? Confirmation comes via a scanner that connects to a diagnostic port inside the cabin. Its purpose is to retrieve a code which defines the issue.

If the light indicates a fault consider your next move. If the vehicle is for sale at a dealership there is probably a scanner on site. Can the code be retrieved now? If so, check what it means online. Search by make, model, and code then consider whether the fault is major or minor. Either way, the seller might offer to fix it. Be careful. The scanner can cancel the light irrespective of whether the work has been completed. If, therefore, the fault is intermittent the light might not reappear for hours, days, or weeks. By then you might own the vehicle.

Cleaned

The internal combustion engine is a large, smelly, fossil fuel burning monster that is exposed to every kind of dirt and weather. Over time and mileage, such things take a toll on its appearance. That is not typically a problem. Too clean is more of a worry. Why? Because perhaps someone cleaned it with a high pressure hose. This is common. If so, was enough care taken to cover the electrical parts with plastic or were they soaked? Furthermore, did this work remove evidence of a leak? It can be difficult to answer such questions, but if the engine looks unusually clean question the seller accordingly.

On the Road

Note how the engine behaves while the car is in motion. Does it work smoothly and consistently, or lose power? Does it cut out? Does it nearly cut out? Furthermore, consider whether the car accelerates at a suitable pace. What is suitable varies, of course. A nearly new, high performance coupé is supposed to be fast whereas a city car can barely drag itself off the driveway. Does the performance feel right, then? If there is cause for concern, it might be practical to test another car for comparison that has the same engine and transmission. Does it feel better or worse? Does it feel the same? A franchise dealership often has several examples of the same model.

Automatic Engine Stop and Start

This system switches the engine off while the vehicle is stationary. While you wait at a red traffic light, for instance. Its purpose is to save fuel and reduce pollution. It might only work once the engine is warm, though. To test it, ensure the system is on then drive a short distance. The next steps are dependant on the type of gearbox. If the car is an automatic:

- stop and keep your foot on the brake pedal
- ensure the engine turns off

- release the brake pedal
- confirm the engine starts.

If the car has manual transmission:

- stop
- select neutral
- release the clutch pedal
- check the engine goes off
- press the clutch pedal
- confirm the engine comes on.

Check List 4: Vehicle Inspection

Factor 13: Engine Start Battery

Consider the Supporting Material that follows, then check the battery that helps start the engine and list any worries.

Check List 4: Vehicle Inspection

Factor 13: Engine Start Battery

Supporting Material

The battery provides the electricity required to start the internal combustion engine. It is then recharged by the alternator. The first step of the inspection is to find the battery and estimate its age. It is likely in the engine bay or behind a carpeted panel in the boot. Does the battery look new or older than a dinosaur's birth certificate? Naturally, it is more likely to look old if it sits by the engine. Proof of age might come via a sticker or heat stamp that incorporates a code. Hopefully any code is easy to read. 12 19 might be December 2019, for example. If the code is obscure the internet might help.

Furthermore, look for a sticker that confirms the length of the warranty. 3 to 5 years is likely. This implies how long the manufacturer expects the battery to last at a minimum. Naturally, it might last longer or fail prematurely if life has been tough. Regular exposure to low temperature takes its toll, for example. Is the car from a cold climate? There might also be a circular, colour coded indicator that implies whether the battery is healthy. Note too that the battery contains acid so ensure this unpleasant, corrosive liquid is sealed within rather than leaking. Further look for corrosion on the positive and negative terminals. Such issues can impede performance.

Start the engine to check the battery further. Does it start easily? If it is sluggish the battery is probably weak. This assumes there are no other contributing factors. In contrast, perhaps the engine refuses to fire but you hear the starter motor click repeatedly. The battery can cause this issue, too. Alternatively, if the engine starts nicely switch it off. Now repeat the test twice more. If the battery is healthy and nicely charged, it can easily start the engine several times in quick succession. Now, let the engine run so the battery can charge.

Check List 4: Vehicle Inspection

Factor 14: Engine Cooling

Consider the Supporting Material that follows, then check the engine cooling system and note any problems.

Check List 4: Vehicle Inspection

Factor 14: Engine Cooling

Supporting Material

The cooling system has to work properly as it stops the engine overheating. The vehicle might breakdown in this circumstance. Core components include the radiator which is large, rectangular, and full of coolant. This mixture of water and antifreeze is pumped throughout the engine via metal channels and rubber hoses.

The first step of the inspection is to find the radiator. It is probably at the front of the engine bay if the car does not have air conditioning. Why so far forward? Because air then hits it as you drive and cools the coolant. In contrast, if the car has air conditioning the condenser (more on that later) is probably at the front of the bay. The radiator is likely behind the condenser. Both look similar so it is easy to mistake them. Note too that the radiator has hundreds of small, wavy fins that optimise efficiency. Ensure the vast majority of the fins are present. Also look for leaks, dents, and any other problem.

Furthermore, there is likely a fan immediately next to the radiator. Its purpose is to further cool the coolant. With the engine off unless you want your fingers removed, confirm the blades are present and in good condition. Note cracks, for instance.

The radiator also has a pressure relief cap so inspect its perimeter for leaks. The next step might be to remove the cap but be very, very careful. Why? Because the cooling system works at high pressure and the liquid within gets very, very hot. Removing the cap might therefore let this burning, high pressure liquid escape at high speed. Expect to get showered and injured. The key is to only remove the radiator cap if the engine is stone cold. There is then less pressure. If the cap can be removed safely inspect the rubber seal for cracks, splits, and an overly rigid texture. Further ensure that the spring in the cap expands and contracts. Best squeeze it to be certain.

There is more to consider. Note the large, easy to see, rubber hose that runs to the top of the radiator. Assuming it is not hotter than the surface of the sun, squeeze it to assess its texture. Crusty implies it has seen better days. Also look for cracks, leaks, and ensure the clamps that hold it both ends are secure. Repeat the checks for the lower hose if you can get to it.

Furthermore, refer to the manual if necessary then find the coolant reservoir in the engine bay. Now check its level via the minimum and maximum marks. If the level is low there might be a leak. Best also note the colour of the coolant in the reservoir. It might be green, orange, or something else depending on the specification. Once identified, see if it is sprayed around the engine bay. Note also that coolant can congeal, stick, and be tricky to remove. Such characteristics might help you spot a leak.

Naturally, the best test of the cooling system is to run the engine to see if it overheats. Simply note the temperature gauge on the dashboard during your test drive. Does the needle stay far below the red line? Somewhere close to the middle is reassuring but make some allowance if you live in a hot climate. Confirm too that the temperature gauge rises beyond minimum. If it sticks to the bottom there is a problem.

Check List 4: Vehicle Inspection

Factor 15: Clutch and Transmission

Consider the Supporting Material that follows, then check the clutch and transmission and list any faults.

Check List 4: Vehicle Inspection

Factor 15: Clutch and Transmission

Supporting Material

Clutch For Manual Transmission

The clutch operates via the pedal on your extreme left. Its purpose is to connect and disconnect the engine to the transmission so you can change gear. Simply press the pedal to disconnect a gear from the engine, pick its replacement then release the pedal. To test the clutch, start the engine and press the pedal all the way to the floor. Does it move easily and smoothly? If you have to stamp on it with both feet there might be a fault. A sticky clutch cable, perhaps. Confirm too that the pedal returns to its former, higher position once it is released.

Furthermore, note that the connection between the engine and transmission comes via a high friction surface in the clutch. This surface wears with mileage. Once the wear is significant, the engine and transmission cannot form a tight seal. This problem is called clutch slip and is easy to recognise. How? Simply change from second gear to third as you drive. Now quickly release the clutch pedal and press the throttle firmly. Does the car accelerate immediately? If the engine revolutions rise without any meaningful increase in speed - as if the transmission is in neutral - the clutch is probably on its way out. Further note any burning smell.

Manual Transmission

Check the transmission carefully as faults can be expensive to repair. First start the car and pick a gear. Now wobble the stick from side to side. How much does it move? Some movement is fine, but if it is excessive there might be a fault. Perhaps the linkage that connects the stick to the transmission is past its best. Check a few gears for peace of mind. Also move up and down the transmission. Go, for example, from first to second, second to third, and fifth to third. Remember reverse. Ensure throughout that the mechanism feels positive, smooth, and that there is no need for excess force. In other words, confirm that it is easy to select all the gears. Repeat this process during your test drive.

There is more to consider as you drive. Ensure that once a gear is selected it remains so until you pick a replacement. A range of faults might make it jump into neutral. Worn transmission mounts, for example. Also listen for whining, banging, and/or growling noises that imply a bill is on its way.

Automatic Transmission

To test the automatic transmission put your foot on the brake pedal, start the engine, and slide the stick to drive (D). Is a gear now available immediately? Can the car move immediately, in other words? Any delay is a concern. Repeat this test for reverse gear (R). Now switch back to drive and cruise to 40 miles per hour. This speed likely enables the transmission to reach its top gear. Does the transmission climb nicely up the gears? Note any rough changes, late changes, and slips that feel like it is in neutral. Listen too. Can you hear banging, whining, and/or growling? Now slow down and stop. Does your transmission move nicely down its gears?

Furthermore, cruise back to 40 miles per hour. Now work the transmission harder. Kick down, in other words. This fast, sudden stamp on the throttle tells it you need a sudden burst of speed rather than a gradual rise. As the transmission is likely in top gear, expect it to drop a couple to facilitate. Does it? There might be a readout that confirms what gear is selected. If not, feel and listen to the car. In contrast, the transmission might only drop a single gear if you accelerate gently.

There is more to consider. Once it is safe, brake hard enough to lose a lot of speed in a fairly short distance. Does the transmission react properly? In other words, is the car ready to accelerate the moment you step back on the throttle? The purpose of these tests is to prove the transmission quickly, consistently, and smoothly picks a suitable gear for the scenario.

The transmission likely has manual selection, too. This ensures that some, or all, of its gears can be engaged based on your preference rather than what it thinks is best. Manual selection comes via the stick and/or paddles behind the steering wheel. Ensure the controls work. However, note that the transmission might refuse some manual selections on safety grounds. It is dangerous to go from sixth to first at high speed, for instance.

Furthermore, if the transmission has a dipstick remove it to inspect the oil. Why? Because the level might be wrong. Too little causes issues such as overheating, rough changes, and slow engagement. The transmission might slip too. In contrast, if there is too much oil it might be whipped into foam and not circulate properly.

To check the oil, the transmission likely has to be at working temperature but this is not universally true. Furthermore, there is no single rule for whether the vehicle has to be switched on or off. On this basis, refer to the manual or the internet for any specifics. Now follow the required steps and:

- stop on a flat surface
- put the transmission in park (P)
- confirm the parking brake is on
- open the bonnet
- remove the dipstick
- wipe off any oil that might provide a false reading

- replace the dipstick
- retrieve the dipstick again
- take a reading via the high and low marks
- replace the dipstick.

Note too that new transmission oil tends to be red and transparent. It then gets darker with mileage. Furthermore, a burning smell suggests there is too much friction within the transmission. It suggests it is overheating, in other words. Be worried. Bad transmission is a great reason to sell the vehicle.

Check List 4: Vehicle Inspection

Factor 16: Exhaust

Consider the Supporting Material that follows, then check the exhaust and list any issues.

Check List 4: Vehicle Inspection

Factor 16: Exhaust

Supporting Material

The exhaust allows waste material from the engine's combustion process to escape the confines of the car. This long, metal, mostly tubular system also incorporates parts that minimise noise and pollution. It likely runs from the engine to the exit point(s) close to the rear bumper. To test it, note that the exhaust gets very, very hot once the engine is switched on. It then stays hot for a considerable time once it is off. Best wear heat resistant gloves if you touch the exhaust.

Start the inspection at the rear of the exhaust. Confirm first that it is securely attached to the car and in the correct position. If it hangs too low the support bracket might be broken. Alternatively, the exhaust itself might be in pieces. Visual observation and gently prodding provide the necessary insight. Look too for cracks and holes that let waste material escape prematurely. These faults might be outlined by black carbon. Also check for serious corrosion that suggests this section of exhaust is past its best. Finally, follow the exhaust forward and repeat these checks for any parts you can see.

Now start the engine and listen for anything that suggests the exhaust leaks. If it is very loud there might be a significant flaw. A large crack, for example. In contrast a low, burbling growl might imply there is a small hole. Either way, press the throttle to emphasise such issues. Life is not that simple, though. Note then that there is no universal optimum tone for exhaust systems. A powerful coupé is supposed to roar like a lion but the same cannot be said for a cheap, basic city car. The latter is supposed to whimper and get bullied by tougher vehicles.

On this basis, if you cannot be certain whether the exhaust

leaks consider the vehicle in a wider context. Is it a cheap, basic supermini that has no sporty credentials whatsoever? Is it old? Is the exhaust rusty? If so, it might be reasonable to conclude there is more likely a leak. In contrast, it might be sensible to give a nearly new sports car the benefit of the doubt.

There is more to consider. The MOT requires the exhaust to be complete so the car is quiet and environmentally friendly. See first whether the muffler that deadens the engine noise is present. Can you see this big, rectangular item forward of the exit point(s)? If not, perhaps someone removed it to make the car roar. I knew someone that drilled a hole in his for this reason.

And what about any diesel particulate filter that reduces pollution? The examiner expects it to be present. But what if it broke? What if it was then removed but not replaced? This is possible if the car's keeper wanted to save money. The issue is that it can be tricky to prove the filter is present. Clever welding can conceal any removal. At one time, this was a common trick. Maybe question the seller and judge the reaction.

Heat Shields

There are likely several heat shields immediately above the exhaust. On this basis, if a shield is loose it might drop, strike the exhaust, and rattle like a tin can. The noise might be intrusive. So, choose a shield to check first. It probably resembles a thin, flexible sheet of metal. Consider now whether it is secure or hanging by a thread. The latter is probable if the bolts are rusty (as is common). If required, poke it to prove all is well. Repeat this process for any other shield.

Check List 4: Vehicle Inspection

Factor 17: Brakes

Consider the Supporting Material that follows, then evaluate the brakes and jot down any problems.

Check List 4: Vehicle Inspection

Factor 17: Brakes

Supporting Material

Brake System Visual Inspection

The brake system comes in handy if you want to stop. The alternative is to throw an anchor out the window and hope for the best. To start the test, peer through the spokes of the front right wheel (if possible). Now consider the condition of the brake. It likely incorporates a circular disc that has a smooth, shiny face. Is the disc in good condition? Note scoring and corrosion. Further signs of wear include a lip around the edge that is easier to feel than see. If, therefore, the disc is cool put your fingertip on its face then slide it towards the outer edge. The larger the lip the more the wear. Millimetres are signifiant.

Now find the calliper which is a large, easy to see, metal claw that grips the disc. It contains inner and outer pads. As you brake, the calliper pushes the pads against the disc and the car slows. The pads wear with mileage. Note that the edge of the outer pad might be visible through the wheel. Can you estimate its thickness? If the pad is brand new it is likely about 16 millimetres. Go wheel to wheel and repeat this procedure.

Note: Alternatively, the car has drum brakes at its rear. This is more probable if it is old and/or basic. In this scenario, there are no discs to inspect and the pads (shoes) cannot be seen without disassembly.

Brake Performance

Check too how the system performs. This is easy. Simply find a straight, flat, quiet road that has very little camber to distort the test. Now drive at 30 miles per hour, keep the steering straight, and brake lightly. Does the vehicle lose speed at a suitable pace without pulling to the left or right? If it pulls, perhaps a calliper is misbehaving, e.g. not applying enough pressure. Also note any peculiar feelings through the pedal. Warped discs cause vibration, for example. Further listen for strange noises. Grinding implies the pads are thinner than a receding hairline. If the system works well, repeat the test at higher speed and brake a little firmer. Be careful not to skid.

Antilock Brake System

The antilock brake system makes the car less likely to skid. To check all is well, look for a message on the dashboard that says there is a fault. Any additional practical test is too risky. Why? Because it requires you to try to force a skid and see what happens. If the system is faulty you might skid into something costly. There is a theoretical procedure, though. So:

- find a straight, quiet, flat road with minimal camber
- position the car so there is room to its front, left, and right to recover if the antilock fails
- drive at no more than 25 miles per hour
- keep the steering wheel straight
- ensure there is no traffic behind
- brake hard enough to make the system react
- expect the brake pedal to pulse
- check the car stops without skidding.

Note: The antilock cannot necessarily stop every skid. Best not rely on it completely.

Adaptive Brake Light System

If you brake hard, this system makes the corresponding lights flash to warn other drivers to react accordingly. The hazard lights flash, too. As hard braking can be risky it is safer not to test the system. However, there is a theoretical process. So:

- find a straight, quiet, flat road with minimal camber
- accelerate to no more than 25 miles per hour
- position the car so there is room to its front, left, and right to recover if you have a problem
- ensure there is no traffic behind
- brake hard
- confirm via the dashboard that the hazard lights flash.

Autonomous Emergency Braking

This system monitors the distance between the front of your car and hazards. Expect a warning if the gap becomes short relative to how much space is required to stop. If you fail to react to the warning, it brakes on your behalf to avoid an impact or mitigate its severity. Clearly, this system cannot be tested safely. However, if it happens to come to life of its own volition you know it works. More practically, look for a warning message on the dashboard which confirms there is a problem.

Emergency Brake Assist

This feature reduces your stopping distance if there is an emergency. It works on the premise that in this scenario you brake very, very quickly but not hard enough. In other words, you move your foot quickly from the throttle to the brake pedal but press the latter too lightly. On this basis, the system recognises your fast footwork and increases the brake pressure. Clearly, it cannot practically be tested. How can you brake then conclude the system shortened the stopping distance? Best look for a message that reveals there is a fault.

Mechanical Parking Brake

The mechanical parking brake incorporates a lever that operates some of the brakes via a cable. The rear brakes only, for instance. Find the lever to start the test. It is likely between the front seats, on the floor left of the pedals, or on the dashboard. There is a slim chance it is by the driver's door. Now:

- stop on a steep hill
- apply the parking brake
- put the transmission into neutral
- swallow a brave pill
- release the brake pedal (be ready to reapply if needed)
- ensure the car stays on its spot.

Further consider how far the lever travels before it is comfortably tight and the car is secure. Too much suggests there is a fault with the cable, for example. Maybe it snapped or stretched. But how much travel is too much? It is tricky to give a definitive answer as cars vary. However, my parking brake is between the front seats, well adjusted, and rises 5 clicks before it is fully engaged. That is a sensible benchmark.

Electric Parking Brake

The electric parking brake works automatically. To test it, park on a hill and listen for a brief, electronic buzz as the motors engage. Further confirmation comes via a light on the dashboard. Now put the transmission in neutral, release the brake pedal, and ensure the car stays on its spot. Now try to move forward. Does the parking brake release automatically? Also, you can set the parking brake manually. The button is likely near to the gear stick or on the dashboard. Does it work?

Brake Pad Wear Indicator System

The brake pad wear indicator system is tricky to test on the forecourt. There is hope, though. Perhaps you know the pads are thin. This is possible if you saw them through the spokes of the wheels (see Brake System Visual Inspection). In this circumstance it is sensible to expect a warning. Is there? In contrast, maybe you know for sure the pads are new. Perhaps they look it. Maybe there is paperwork to prove it. In this circumstance, a warning message to the contrary is a concern.

Check List 4: Vehicle Inspection

Factor 18: Steering

Consider the Supporting Material that follows, then check the steering and list any faults.

Check List 4: Vehicle Inspection

Factor 18: Steering

Supporting Material

Test the steering on a straight, quiet, flat road that has very little camber to distort the result. Now drive at 30 miles per hour with a light grip on the wheel. The light grip makes it easier to feel imperfection. Does the vehicle cruise in a straight line without pulling to the left or right? A pull suggests there is a problem. On this basis, consider whether the steering is fighting or cooperating. If the former, repeat the test elsewhere to check the car is at fault rather than the road.

If the car is to blame there might be a problem with its alignment, i.e. the position of the wheels relative to other relevant components. Never fear, though. This is not a major issue. The likely solution is adjustment rather than repair. However, poor alignment might make the tyres wear unevenly so there can be associated expense. In contrast, perhaps the pull on the steering is caused by a problem with the:

- brakes
- suspension
- tyres
- wheel balance.

Power Steering

Power steering makes it easier to turn the wheel. To test it, drive very, very slowly and turn the steering far left. Now turn it far right. Suspect a problem if these movements require a lot of physical effort. Now increase speed and drive through a few corners. Is the steering slow to react? If so, perhaps the pump that circulates the fluid is past its best. A whining noise implies it is. As for the fluid itself, open the bonnet and check the high and low markers on the reservoir. Is the level appropriate? If not, perhaps there is a leak so look for oil in the engine bay, on the underside of the car, and on the ground.

Manual Steering Wheel Adjustment

This system lets you move the steering wheel to a suitable position. To start the test, release the clamp close to your knees that holds the wheel in position. Now consider the height adjustment. Does the steering wheel move up and down? Further check the reach adjustment. Does the wheel move forward and backward? Confirm too that there is a position that is comfortable and does not block your view of the instruments. Can you see all of the speedometer, for example? Finally, lock the clamp and check the wheel is secure.

Electric Steering Wheel Adjustment

See Manual Steering Wheel Adjustment. In contrast, the electric wheel moves via a motor so there is no manual clamp to release. Check the wheel is secure in its current position to start the test. I once saw someone manually lift an electric wheel to its highest spot. It then crashed to its lowest once released. Also confirm the wheel moves in every direction via its motor. In addition, it might automatically rise to its highest spot as you turn the vehicle off. This is not likely a fault. It is more likely making extra room for you to get out. Does the steering wheel go back to its former spot as you restart the car?

Heated Steering Wheel

The heated steering wheel keeps your hands warm on cold days. To ensure the test is fair, first touch the outside of the wheel to prove it is cool. Baked by the sun is no use. Now activate the heater, wait a while, then touch the same parts of the wheel. Are they warmer? Expect the centre and any buttons to remain cool.

Check List 4: Vehicle Inspection

Factor 19: Suspension

Consider the Supporting Material that follows, then check the suspension and jot down any worries.

Check List 4: Vehicle Inspection

Factor 19: Suspension

Supporting Material

The car has to be lifted to properly inspect the suspension. Never fear, though. You can still make useful observations on the ground. The first step is to park on a flat surface, straighten the steering, and consider how the car sits. Now note the size of the gap between the top of the front, right tyre and the wheel arch. Compare it to the front left. Any inconsistency implies something is wrong. So does insufficient clearance. Naturally, repeat this test for the rear of the vehicle. Only compare front to front and rear to rear, though. My car sits slightly lower at the rear but its suspension is fine.

Now return to the front right corner. Can you see a large coil spring as you peer around the tyre? If helpful, turn the steering wheel to full lock to optimise your view. The purpose of the spring is to expand and contract to absorb bumps in the road. Note its condition. Is it broken, e.g. snapped? Also look for any significant corrosion that suggests it is past its best.

In addition, look within the spring for a long tubular shock absorber. Its purpose is to limit the movement of the spring to improve the vehicle’s handling. Note that the shock absorber contains oil that leaks if there is a fault. Can you see oil along its length? Furthermore, oil travels so evaluate any nearby components. Is there oil on the spring, for example? Also check the ground. My shock absorber once leaked all over the drive. I was thrilled. Recognise too that the absorber is partly surrounded by a rubber boot that keeps it clean and extends its life. Note the condition of this boot. Is it complete or has it fallen apart?

Also consider how the suspension behaves while the car is stationary. This is straightforward. Simply put your hands on the corner then push up and down a few times to make the suspension bounce. Now stop and see how long it takes to settle completely. A bounce and a half is a reasonable benchmark that suggests all is well. In contrast, if it bounces too long the shock absorber might be past its best. Be careful not to damage the car. If you push too hard you might dent it.

Naturally, the suspension incorporates other components that are tricky to see clearly without lifting the car. However, if you catch a glimpse look for rust on anything metal and splits on anything rubber. Whereas such parts can look bad but work perfectly, these observations create an overall impression. Does the suspension look brand new, for example? Or does it look like it spent a year at the bottom of the sea? Be suspicious if you spot a fish. Finally, move throughout the vehicle and repeat your checks.

Note: Shock absorbers can also be found close to coil springs rather than within them. In contrast, if the car is old it might have leaf spring suspension at its rear rather than coil. A leaf incorporates a long, narrow strip of curved metal that has shorter equivalents attached below. It resembles a banana. Pick a leaf to start the inspection. Can you see any breaks or serious corrosion? Now move to the other leaf to repeat.

On the Road

Driving the vehicle further reveals whether the suspension is about to raid your pension fund. However, note that what is optimum varies. A stiff, sporty coupé has different optimum characteristics than a luxury saloon, for example. The former prioritises handling whereas the latter favours comfort. That said, if the vehicle is reasonably modern certain behaviour implies imperfection whatever its class. Issues to note include:

- nose dives if you brake firmly
- crashes through small imperfections in the road

- leans so hard in corners that the mirrors hit the tarmac.

Air Suspension

There are contrasting considerations if the vehicle has air suspension rather than coil or leaf spring. For starters, a compressor forces air into a bellow at each wheel. These bellows help maintain the vehicle's ride height. Go wheel to wheel and look for damage, then. Note for instance rips, cracks, and holes. Furthermore, start the vehicle and give the bellows a few seconds to fill with air if required. Now note anything that suggests there is a fault. For example:

- hissing noise as air escapes
- vehicle sits unevenly
- suspension takes too long to rise
- compressor noisier than a rock concert
- warning message on the dashboard
- sound of money pouring out your wallet.

Check List 4: Vehicle Inspection

Factor 20: Electric Drive Motor

Consider the Supporting Material that follows, then evaluate the electric motor and list any concerns.

Check List 4: Vehicle Inspection

Factor 20: Electric Drive Motor

Supporting Material

How an Electric Motor Works

The motor converts electrical energy from the vehicle's battery to mechanical energy that spins its wheels. But how? In its basic form, an electric motor contains a fixed, permanently on magnet that is shaped like a horseshoe. This magnet has a positive and negative pole. The positive pole repels the positive of any other magnet and simultaneously attracts the negative. Its negative does the opposite. Note too that the horseshoe shape means there is a gap between the poles. The armature sits in this gap. What it the armature, you say? It is a rotating coil of wire that conducts electricity. Electricity flows from the vehicle's battery, enters the armature and creates a second magnetic field within the motor.

The magnetic field from the armature now interacts with its counterpart from the horseshoe magnet. The poles attract and repel, in other words. These forces make the armature spin but only about half a turn. Why half? Because the armature positive stops close to the horseshoe negative. In contrast, the armature negative stops close to the horseshoe positive. The magnetic forces ensure it. But this limited movement is no use in a motor. At best, it can only propel your car slightly forward.

The solution is the commutator that is connected to the armature and rotates with it. Its purpose is to regularly reverse the direction electricity flows through the armature. This process reverses the magnetic poles. In other words, the armature positive becomes armature negative and the armature negative becomes armature positive. This exchange ensures the magnetic field from the armature repels and attracts its counterpart in the fixed, permanently active horseshoe magnet in a way that lets the armature spin constantly in the same direction.

How to Test the Drive Motor

As you can see, the vehicle's electric motor is mechanically simple so there is not a lot to break. It is far simpler than a petrol engine, for example. However, look for a warning message on the dashboard which suggests it is about to expire. Naturally, confirm that the vehicle moves too. Now listen to the electric motor as you drive. Expect it to whine a bit but ensure the noise is not too intrusive. If it is, perhaps the bearing that supports the armature is on borrowed time. When you lift the throttle, a worn bearing can sound like a circular saw grinding to a halt. If you suspect the bearing is noisy but cannot be sure, test other such cars for comparison.

Check List 4: Vehicle Inspection

Factor 21: Electric Vehicle Battery

Consider the Supporting Material that follows, then check the battery that powers the electric motor and note any issues.

Check List 4: Vehicle Inspection

Factor 21: Electric Vehicle Battery

Supporting Material

Battery Performance

To recap, the car's motor is powered by a battery that has a capacity, i.e. the amount of electricity it stores. Imagine the battery is brand new and fully charged. Perhaps the vehicle therefore has a maximum range of 200 miles (in laboratory conditions). However, the capacity of the battery falls with age and mileage. The battery effectively gets smaller, in other words. On this basis, even if it is fully charged the vehicle's range is less than when it left the factory. That can be annoying.

To fully evaluate the health of the battery you need a professional with specialised equipment. However, there is hope on the forecourt. Check first for a warning message on the dashboard that suggests it is at the end of its life. In addition, there might be a dial that reveals whether the battery's capacity has diminished. An ever shortening line, for example. Do not confuse a capacity dial with a charge dial. In addition, the car might be compatible with a smartphone application that - its makers say - provides insight. Can you find an application that might live up to the hype? Is it worth a look?

Naturally, the vehicle might not have a capacity dial or be compatible with a smartphone application. In this circumstance, the only way to evaluate the battery is to see how it performs on the road. This requires you to compare the vehicle's current maximum range to its maximum when it left the factory. The brochure confirms the latter and is likely available online. However, the manufacturer's figure is probably the best case scenario - so do some more research via online forums. What do owners of this type of vehicle realistically manage on real roads with a new battery? Now:

- ensure the battery is fully charged
- set the vehicle to its most economical mode
- drive a tenth of the realistic maximum range
- note how much charge is left in the battery.

If the battery performs like new it might be 90 percent charged after your drive. If it is, you might reasonably conclude there is no cause for concern. Good! But what if the battery is at 80 percent? Or 75? Is it past its best? Maybe. Maybe not. Why? Because your driving style, the type of roads, and other factors influenced how much power was consumed. Perhaps you consistently drove uphill into a headwind. That took more power than cruising on the flat in calm weather. Perhaps low temperature hindered the battery's performance, too. There are a lot of variables. Be prudent, though. If, on balance, there is cause for concern it might be sensible to have the battery assessed professionally.

Charging

The vehicle is little more than an ornament if it cannot be charged, so check all is well. Simply find a public charger, a manufacturer home charger, or any standard socket. Now:

- check you can open the flap that covers the charge socket
- confirm the cable connects securely to said socket
- ensure the opposite end of the cable is connected to power
- press whatever buttons are required to start the charge
- check the indicator in the car confirms it is charging.

Furthermore, ensure the vehicle continues to charge unless

there is a valid reason for it to stop. The valid reasons include:

- battery is full
- payment issue
- power cut.

If the car cannot charge properly consider why. Maybe there is a mechanical fault or it needs new software. Perhaps instead the cable itself is broken. Repeat the test with a different cable if necessary. Furthermore, it is possible the charger is faulty.

Check List 4: Vehicle Inspection

Factor 22: Hybrid and Plug-in Hybrid Drive Battery

Consider the Supporting Material that follows, then list any concerns that relate to the hybrid battery.

Check List 4: Vehicle Inspection

Factor 22: Hybrid and Plug-in Hybrid Drive Battery

Supporting Material

Performance

To recap, the car is propelled by its internal combustion engine and an electric motor. The former is powered by petrol or diesel, and the latter by a battery. In some circumstances, the motor propels the car single-handed to save fuel. This is most probable when its power consumption is low. While travelling slowly in town, for example. At other times, the electric motor and engine combine to maximise power which is handy if you need a burst of speed. Note too that the battery has a capacity, i.e. how much electricity it can store. This capacity diminishes with age and mileage so the battery effectively gets smaller. It is then capable of less work per charge.

To test the battery properly, it has to be connected to a tool not many people have. However, certain behaviour you can observe might imply the battery is past its best. For example:

- engine often runs when it is fair to expect the motor to propel the car single-handed, e.g. in town at low speed
- warning message on the dashboard
- high fuel consumption (refer to the trip computer)
- battery charge falls quickly.

Charging

If the car is a hybrid – rather than a plug-in hybrid – its battery is only charged by the internal combustion engine. Is there a message on the dashboard that suggests this is not happening? In contrast, if it is a plug-in it can also be recharged like an electric car. Via a socket and cable, in other words. See Check List 4 Factor 21: Electric Vehicle Battery.

Check List 4: Vehicle Inspection

Factor 23: Seats

Consider the Supporting Material that follows, then check the seats and list any faults.

Check List 4: Vehicle Inspection

Factor 23: Seats

Supporting Material

Manual Seats

Manual seats have to be moved into position by hand, so there is no electrical assistance. Start the test at the driver's seat. Note first whether it fulfils its primary purpose. Sit then. Is the seat comfortable or an instrument of torture? Ensure too that it is level. If a support rail is broken it might lean to the side. If the seat is uncomfortable now imagine how you might feel after a long journey. You might need a chiropractor. Also, evaluate the fabric and/or leather. The issues to note include:

- tears
- burst stitches
- scuffs
- holes
- stains
- cigarette burns
- cracks
- excessive dirt.

Now check the seat moves. Naturally, the primary adjustment is forward and backward. Does it slide smoothly in both directions then lock in position? If it cannot move at all perhaps the mechanism is wrecked. If it cannot move far enough perhaps there is a less serious issue. A blockage, for example. Repeat this procedure for any other directions of travel such as tilt, height, and lumber. As for the headrest, you might have to release a clamp on its leg before it moves up and down. Check the vehicle's remaining seats as appropriate.

Electric Seats

See Manual Seats for the initial insight. In contrast, pick an electric seat and confirm it moves smoothly, reliably, and without issue via its motor. Move about the cabin and repeat.

Memory Seats

Start the inspection at the driver’s seat. Can you see buttons such as 1, 2, and 3? Each button relates to a preset, user specified position that the seat remembers. Now move the seat to an unusual position that nobody is likely to want. Extremely close to the steering wheel with an enormous forward tilt, for example. Now press button 1. Does the seat move automatically to a sensible spot? If so, happy days. If not, there is a fault or no preset position. To prove which, make a preset and try again. Repeat the process for the other buttons, e.g. 2 and 3. Finally, go from seat to seat as required.

Heated Seats

A heated seat contains components that warm some parts of its surface. The back support and horizontal cushion, perhaps. Check the driver's first then move throughout the cabin. The process is:

- touch the seat and note its temperature
- set the heater to full power to provide the best contrast
- wait a minute
- touch the seat on the same spots and check it is warm.

Ventilated Seats

A ventilated seat contains fans that circulate air around its surface. This keeps you cooler on hot days. To start the test, squat by the driver's seat and engage full power so the sensation is at its most noticeable. Now put your hand on the seat and ensure you feel a breeze. Go seat to seat and repeat.

Massaging Seats

A massaging seat is the most annoying invention known to mankind. It mimics being kidnapped by aliens, taken to a spaceship, and probed in a deeply personal manner. On this basis, it incorporates air pockets that repeatedly fill and empty. This rolling movement massages your back, hips, and other parts that fascinate little green men from Mars! Sit in the driver's seat to start your inspection. Now engage the most vigorous setting. Do you feel violated and inclined to call for help? If so, the pockets are probably airtight. Best run through any softer settings, too. Now go seat to seat and repeat.

Active Headrests

Whiplash is a neck injury caused by the sudden, sharp movement of your head. The active headrest reduces this issue. It therefore moves forward to limit how far your head can travel if there is a collision. Start the inspection at the driver's headrest. Do you think it deployed? Check carefully as it is important to spot anything that suggests the car crashed.
Note first that the headrest might have a front and rear that separate if there is a collision. High pressure gas might facilitate this process. Is there separation? In contrast, the headrest might not separate and operate via a lever in the seat. If so, your body weight transfers through the seat and pushes the lever. It is harder to spot this type of deployment but check the trim at the bottom of the headrest's legs. Does it look out of position? Finally, go from seat to seat and repeat.

Folding Rear Seat System

This system lets the vertical back support of the bench fold against the horizontal cushion as a single piece. Luggage too big for the boot can then stretch into the cabin. Clearly, the primary concern is that the bench is secure once positioned for passengers. If not, it might leap forward if you brake hard and injure somebody. Pull and push to confirm all is well. Also:

- operate the clamps to ensure they release
- confirm the back support folds flat
- return the back support to its former position
- ensure the clamps engage.

Split and Fold Rear Seat System

See Folding Rear Seat System. In contrast, the vertical back support is not a single piece so it splits by percentage. 60-40 or 40-20-40, for example. Best check each section in isolation.

Occasional Third Row Seating System

This seating emerges from the floor of the boot. To test it, operate whatever clamps, hinges, or straps are necessary to position it for passengers. Is it now secure? Pull it to make sure. Now check it returns to the stowed position without issue.

Tumbling Seats

A tumbling seat makes it easier to carry large, awkward luggage. It can therefore be moved out the way as required. Choose a seat to start the inspection. Is it secure once positioned for a passenger? Best pull it to make sure. Furthermore, does the back support fold flat against the horizontal cushion without issue? Does the whole lot now roll forward into the floor well to make additional space behind for your luggage? Note too that it might scuff any seat ahead. Is there any damage? Move now from seat to seat and repeat.

Removable Seats

See Tumbling Seats for the related insight. In contrast, ensure that each relevant seat can be removed to increase cargo capacity.

ISOFIX System

ISOFIX is the fast, simple, and secure means to connect a child seat to the vehicle without wrapping it with a seatbelt. It therefore has anchor points that can be accessed through narrow slots in the car's upholstery. Can you see them close to the seatbelt buckles? Note that the slots can stretch and look ugly. Is there any ugliness? Alternatively, the anchors might be immediately visible or hidden by plastic covers. If the latter, consider whether the covers are broken. Finally, is it worth checking your particular seat fits the car? There is no guarantee.

Check List 4: Vehicle Inspection

Factor 24: Seatbelts

Consider the Supporting Material that follows, then assess the seatbelts and jot down any problems.

Check List 4: Vehicle Inspection

Factor 24: Seatbelts

Supporting Material

Function and Condition

Check the driver's belt first. How? Simply extend its entire length and look for cuts and frays that weaken it. Furthermore, confirm it emerges smoothly. Check it does not repeatedly get stuck, in other words. Now connect the tongue to the buckle. Does it attach without issue? Is it secure? Press the red release button, too. Does the tongue disconnect easily or get stuck? Ensure now that the belt retracts fully into its housing without complaint. Life is tiresome if you have to feed it piece by piece.

Furthermore, put the belt on then grip the part that covers the middle of your chest. Now pull it hard and sharp. Does the belt lock or extend? The former is preferable. Why? Because the lock stops the belt extending if the car crashes. It can then hold you in position which is preferable than rolling around the cabin. Check the height adjustment, too. The mechanism is close to your shoulder. Finally, go from belt to belt and repeat.

Seatbelt Pre-tensioner System

This system removes slack from the belts if the car crashes. You are then pulled tight into your seat which is the best position to benefit from any other safety features. The airbags, for example. Clearly, the system cannot be tested on the forecourt unless you plough through the seller’s office. Best not! Look instead for a message that confirms there is a fault.

Seatbelt Reminder System

In the United Kingdom, the law requires you to wear a belt on public roads (generally). If you forget this system beeps to remind you. The likely trigger is hitting a certain speed. On this basis, you cannot legally test this capability except on private land. There is the other side of the coin, though. The system might wrongly conclude you have forgotten to put a belt on. If so, it beeps even though you are secured. This happened to me. It was infuriating. Best watch and listen for false warnings. Also, if you have a passenger(s) the system might also monitor him/her or them. Does it behave properly?

Check List 4: Vehicle Inspection

Factor 25: Heating, Ventilation, and Air Conditioning

Consider the Supporting Material that follows then test the heating, ventilation, and air conditioning systems and list any faults.

Check List 4: Vehicle Inspection

Factor 25: Heating, Ventilation, and Air Conditioning

Supporting Material

Heating and Cooling System

This system propels warm and cool air throughout the cabin. To test it, start the engine and close the windows and doors. Open the vents too. Now set the system to maximum heat at full speed. Does a strong, warm breeze emerge once the engine is at working temperature? Now swap to maximum cool with the air conditioning switched off. Does cooler air emerge? For these full speed tests, expect the fan to be noisy but ensure it does not sound broken. Also check the less vigorous speed settings. Can you set the fan to slow, for example? Finally, note the controls that let you choose where the air is directed such as mostly at the windscreen or mostly at your face. Evaluate each setting. You might find a vent:

- close to the front right window
- near the front left window
- centre of the dashboard
- below the windscreen
- by the driver's feet
- close to the front passenger's feet
- behind the front centre armrest
- beneath the driver’s seat
- under the front passenger’s seat.

In addition, some vents can be further adjusted to fine-tune airflow. Pick a vent to test first. Now check its fins. Do they move as intended, e.g. far left and far right? Furthermore, confirm that the fins stay in the position you specify. Check they do not revert elsewhere, in other words. This is important. Imagine, for example, that air cannot be fired at the front left window to remove condensation. How can you then see the traffic clearly? Confirm that the vent opens and closes, too. Finally, go from vent to vent to repeat the checks.

Air Conditioning

Air conditioning lowers the temperature in the cabin and doubles as a dehumidifier. Note that it contains refrigerant that circulates through a series of components that predominantly sit in the engine bay. The refrigerant also alternates between a gaseous and liquid state. Cars vary but a representative cycle is:

- compressor receives cool, low pressure refrigerant gas that it squeezes so it becomes a hot, high pressure gas
- gas passes via a pipe to the condenser
- cool airflow around the condenser turns the high pressure, high temperature gas into high pressure liquid
- liquid passes to the receiver dryer
- receiver dryer removes contaminants such as water
- liquid flows to the expansion valve
- liquid expands so its pressure falls
- liquid flows to the evaporator
- liquid boils, turns back into gas, then absorbs heat from the surrounding area that chills the walls of the evaporator
- fan blows the cool air around the evaporator into the cabin.

To test the air conditioning, start the vehicle and close the windows and doors. Now set it to maximum, full power cool and open the vents throughout. Does the emerging air have a frosty bite within a short time? If not, perhaps there is no refrigerant to circulate through the system. This is common as the car only contains so much refrigerant and – much like petrol – it gets consumed over time. It then has to be replaced which is a fairly quick, relatively low cost task. Perceive it more as maintenance than repair.

More concerning is if the refrigerant escaped via a broken component, so open the bonnet and look for issues. Can you see the condenser? It looks similar to the radiator and is likely behind the grille at the front of the engine bay. Look now for holes, dents, and anything else that suggests it leaks. Note, however, that refrigerant can escape from any relevant component. On this basis, a mechanic's typical solution is to put fluorescent dye into the system and see where it emerges. A special light is required to see the dye. In contrast, perhaps the compressor is broken. Best turn on the air conditioning and listen. Do you hear a click as the compressor comes to life?

Note: Air conditioning expels water as its waste product that pools beneath the car, so there is no need to worry if you see any. However, it is risky to make assumptions. Best check any discharge is water rather than something worrying such as coolant.

Cooled Glovebox

The cooled glovebox is connected to the vehicle's air conditioning system. Why? So that you can slightly chill food, drink, and smoking hot copies of this book. To ensure all is well:

- open the glovebox and find the vent
- ensure the vent opens and closes
- leave the vent open
- switch the air conditioning to maximum, full power cool

- wait a minute
- put your hand over the vent to check cool air emerges.

Climate Control

Climate control regulates the heater and air conditioning to maintain whatever temperature you specify. 20 degrees, for example. To test it, close the doors and windows then set a preference that contrasts the existing temperature in the cabin. If it is very cold make it warm, for instance. Ensure for this example that the fan speed increases and warm air emerges (once the vehicle is at working temperature). Now wait for some time. Does the fan slow down as the temperature reaches your preference?

Dual Climate Control

See Climate Control for the initial insight. In addition, dual zone lets you choose separate temperature preferences for the driver and front passenger. 20 and 17 degrees respectively, for instance. However, neither person sits in an isolated bubble so the atmospheres mix. On this basis, dual zone provides some individual control but do not expect miracles. To test the system:

- set the driver's temperature to maximum heat
- make the passenger’s preference far cooler
- put your hand close to a vent that points at the driver
- confirm the emerging air is warm
- move your hand to a vent that points at the passenger
- ensure the air is cooler.

Triple Climate Control

See Climate Control and Dual Climate Control for the initial insight. However, test the separate temperate preferences for the:

- driver
- front passenger
- rear passengers as a single entity.

Quadruple Climate Control

See Climate Control and Dual Climate Control for the initial insight. However, test the separate temperate preferences for the:

- driver
- front passenger
- rear right passenger
- rear left passenger.

Check List 4: Vehicle Inspection

Factor 26: Manoeuvring Aids

Consider the Supporting Material that follows, then evaluate the manoeuvring aids and list any problems.

Check List 4: Vehicle Inspection

Factor 26: Manoeuvring Aids

Supporting Material

Rear Parking Sensor System

The rear parking sensor system helps you judge distance while reversing. It therefore bounces signals off hazards such as walls. Beeps of varying frequency reveal whether the hazard is close, closer, or far too close for comfort. To test it, go to the back of the car and find the circular sensors in its bumper. Ensure each sensor is present, intact, and in the appropriate position. See they are not pushed through the bumper, for example.

Now find a test hazard, i.e. something in close proximity to manoeuvre the vehicle around. To minimise risk, pick something soft and cheap rather than hard and expensive. Now test the sensors in the middle of the bumper. How? Simply reverse straight towards the hazard. Do you hear beeps once it is within a metre? Now move a little bit closer. Do the beeps get faster? Now move closer still. Do the beeps get even faster then become a constant tone? Repeat this test for the sensors at the bumper's corners, i.e. the left and right.

Furthermore, find the picture of the bumper on the vehicle's screen. Can you see lines at the left corner, right corner, and centre? These lines flash and/or change colour to reveal the location of the hazard. This is useful as beeps only reveal the distance to impact. On this basis, ensure the lines react as required. For instance, if the hazard is to your left check the left lines react. Ensure too that the screen is intact and working properly. Note flickering, cutting out, and/or a lack of clarity.

Front Parking Sensor System

See Rear Parking Sensor System for the procedure. In contrast, test:

- front centre
- front left
- front right.

Reversing Camera

The reversing camera makes it easier to see hazards behind the car. To test it, select reverse and ensure the image appears automatically. The screen is in the dashboard, the rear-view mirror, or the virtual cockpit. Confirm too that the picture is clear. Does the screen flicker? If it does there is likely a fault. In contrast, perhaps the image is foggy as the camera lens is covered with condensation. This is inevitable in certain weather. In this scenario, find the camera close to the registration plate. Now clean it and repeat the test. More worrying is condensation on the interior of the camera that proves the weather seal is poor. Such a fault might shorten its lifespan.

Around View Monitor

The around view monitor provides a bird's eye, 360 degree view of the surroundings to make low speed manoeuvres easy. The images come via a camera on each side of the vehicle plus a screen on the dashboard. Expect a picture of the roof and any hazards to your front, rear, left, and right. See Reversing Camera for the test procedure but expand it to cover multiple cameras. Note that your:

- front camera is probably close to the grille
- rear camera is likely near the registration plate
- right camera is likely in the bottom of the right mirror
- left camera is probably in the bottom of the left mirror.

Cruise Control

Cruise control regulates the throttle to maintain your favoured speed. To confirm it works, recognise that it has to be switched on then a second step defines the velocity. So, switch it on. Now accelerate to 30 miles per hour. Why 30? Because the system might not work at very low velocity. Also:

- press the set button to confirm your favoured speed
- release the throttle pedal
- keep an eye on the speedometer
- ensure the car maintains velocity.

There are other points to consider. First, press the throttle to accelerate beyond 30 miles per hour. Now release the throttle pedal. Does the car return to 30 and maintain it? In addition, ensure cruise control disengages the moment you brake or press the cancel button. Now hit resume and ensure the favoured speed is reinstated. Furthermore, the +1 and -1 buttons let you adjust the speed by 1 mile per hour. Check both buttons work.

Finally, note that cruise control might struggle to maintain your specified velocity on steep, downward hills. Why? Because engine braking alone cannot always overcome the immense pull of gravity. So – in this circumstance – there is no reason to conclude there is a fault if the vehicle goes too fast.

Cruise Control With Brake Function

See Cruise Control for the test procedure. In addition, the brake element stops the car accelerating too much on steep, downward hills. The brakes are therefore applied as required. To test this capability, set a speed and go to the top of a long, steep hill. Does the car maintain your preference all the way down?

Adaptive Cruise Control

See Cruise Control for the test procedure. In addition, the adaptive element automatically adjusts your preferred speed to maintain a safe, comfortable distance to the car ahead. To test it:

- leave a large gap to the traffic ahead
- set a speed that is fast enough to close the gap
- ensure your car slows as it approaches the traffic.

Furthermore, there is likely a dial that increases and decreases what constitutes a safe, comfortable distance to the car ahead. You might prefer to stay slightly further back in bad weather, for example. Switch between the closest and furthest settings and check there is a distinguishable difference.

Blind Spot Monitor

Blind spot monitor confirms that a nearby, adjacent vehicle approaching from the rear is hidden by part of your car's bodywork. To test it, find a road that has multiple lanes such as a dual carriageway. Now pass a car on your left. Does, for example, a warning light in the left mirror come on? Does it go out once you pull ahead? Repeat this test for the other mirror.

Rear Cross Traffic Alert

Reversing out a parking bay can be tricky if the cars parked adjacent block your view of any traffic approaching from the sides. This system scans for such hazards via the parking sensors. To prove it works, park nose first in a parking space, select reverse gear, and partly emerge. Now stop and wait for a car. Expect an audible and/or visual alert as it approaches.

Park Assist

This system steers you into parallel and/or perpendicular

parking bays. It might steer out, too. To test it, cruise through a car park or pass a row of vehicles parked next to a kerb. Now engage the system and check it spots a suitable bay, i.e. empty and big enough. Confirmation it has found a bay comes from the audible alert and a message on the dashboard. Now:

- release the steering wheel
- operate the throttle, transmission, and brakes
- follow any further instructions such as move forward
- check the car steers into the parking bay.

Note: You are still responsible for the safety of the car and anything in close proximity. Best not assume the system always makes good decisions. Watch it. Double guess it. Intervene if required.

Hill Assist

This system stops the car rolling back as you start on steep hills. Perhaps you stop at a traffic light, for example. You therefore press – and hold – the brake pedal so the vehicle stays on its spot. However, as the traffic light goes green you move your foot from the brake pedal to the throttle. This releases the brakes so the car rolls back unless you have perfect control of the clutch. Hill assist therefore keeps the brakes engaged for a few extra seconds after you release the pedal. If the car has manual transmission the test procedure is:

- find a steep hill
- brake and bring the car to a halt
- keep your foot on the brake pedal
- leave the parking brake off
- push the clutch pedal to the floor (and hold it)
- release the brake pedal
- ensure the car stays on its spot for a few seconds.

There is a slightly different process if the car has automatic transmission. Once stopped put it in neutral, release the brake pedal, then ensure it remains on the spot for a few seconds.

Lane Departure Warning

Lane departure warning monitors the position of the vehicle relative to the lane marks via a camera. Expect an alert if it wanders off line. Clearly, it is too dangerous to test this system on public roads. However, there is a theoretical procedure that explains the concept. Find a road that has clear marks to get started. Ensure too that there is good visibility. Why? Because snow, fog, and rain compromise performance. Now engage the system and cruise above the speed required for it to work (check the car's manual or the internet to confirm the speed). Perhaps you now accidentally wander over the lane mark. If so expect an audible warning, a message on the dashboard, and/or a vibration in the steering.

Lane Keeping Aid

See Lane Departure Warning for insight. In contrast, expect a slight pull on the steering to nudge you towards the correct lane.

Speed Limiter

The limiter lets you specify a speed the vehicle cannot easily exceed. Excess, gentle throttle pressure cannot then push it above what is legal and/or safe for your scenario. To confirm it works:

- set a limit such as 40 miles per hour
- try to gently accelerate beyond the limit
- ensure the vehicle stays at 40.

That said, there is an override function which is handy if you need a sudden burst of speed. Simply press the throttle hard.

Intelligent Speed Limiter

See Speed Limiter for the test suggestions. In addition, the system adjusts the maximum permitted speed to match the legal limit. It therefore looks for traffic signs via its forward camera. Further confirmation comes from the car's satellite navigation as it knows what road it is on. To check the system:

- find a 40 miles per hour zone, for example
- set 40 as the maximum
- drive at 40
- enter a 30 zone
- ensure the car slows to the lower limit
- go back into the 40 zone
- ensure you can accelerate to the higher limit.

Traction Control

This system intervenes if any driven tyre struggles for traction while you accelerate. How? It reduces engine power and/or applies the relevant brake(s). Clearly, it is not safe to deliberately force this intervention on public roads. However, if the system engages of its own volition there might be a light on the dashboard. Check there is no significant wheel spin in this scenario. Look too for a message that says the system is faulty.

Electronic Stability Control

See Traction Control for the related insight. In contrast, as you corner note any warning message that suggests the electronic stability control is trying to reduce understeer and/or oversteer.

Night Vision

Night vision makes it easier to see people and animals in low light. To confirm it works, check the screen is intact then consider the image. Perhaps you can see a building, a fence, and a creepy garden gnome. Ensure that these lifeless objects are represented by dark colours. Expect various shades of grey. Now point the front of the vehicle towards a person and look at the screen. Is your living helper represented by stronger, brighter colours that vividly contrast the surroundings?

Check List 4: Vehicle Inspection

Factor 27: Collision Protection

Consider the Supporting Material that follows, then check the collision protection systems and list any issues.

Check List 4: Vehicle Inspection

Factor 27: Collision Protection

Supporting Material

Airbag Overview

The car likely has several airbags if it is fairly modern. To test them as a combined entity, start the engine and/or electric motor and check a related light appears on the dashboard (if fitted). Does it vanish a few seconds later? If it stays lit it is indicating a fault. In addition, inspect each airbag to see whether it deployed. This might be easier said than done. Why? Because a good mechanic can replace the airbags and leave little trace of the work. On this basis, look for any poor repair and/or lack of repair based on the ideas below.

Driver Airbag

To deploy, this airbag breaks through a panel in the centre of the steering wheel. Ensure no part of it is visible. Further check the condition of the panel. Is it smashed? It is cracked? Note too that the bag is lubricated by powder. Can you see powder?

Passenger Airbag

See Driver Airbag. In contrast, the passenger airbag breaks through a panel in the dashboard forward of the front passenger.

Side Airbag System

This system protects the driver and front passenger. An airbag therefore emerges from the side of each seat at shoulder height. Go to the driver's seat to start your checks. Now look for the word airbag (or similar) on the side nearest the window. It confirms where the bag is stored. This part of the seat has weak stitches the bag can rip through. So, ensure that you cannot see any part of the bag. Also check the stitches are undamaged. Repeat the checks for the other bag.

Curtain Airbag System

This feature spans the length of the cabin (both sides). The bags sit below the roof yet above the headliner. On this basis, they push past the headliner which makes it fall around its edge. Is the headliner out of position? Is it poorly secured? Is it damaged? Start the inspection by the driver's seat then circumnavigate the vehicle. Furthermore, the bags might extend under the plastic trim on the pillars that help hold the windscreen in position. Does the interior trim look out of place?

Pedestrian Airbag

The airbag emerges from under the bonnet to cover part of the windscreen and the adjacent pillars. So, think back to earlier in the book when you checked the car's bodywork. If you were unable to close the bonnet properly any airbag deployment might have wrecked its hinges. This is a common.

Other Airbags

As relevant, apply the aforementioned checks to any other airbags. Is there protection at the driver's knees, for example?

Passenger Airbag Deactivation System

This system stops the passenger airbag deploying if the car crashes. It cannot then knock a child seat from its safest position. To, for example, switch the bag off insert the car's key into a slot in the glovebox. Now twist. There might instead be a slot in the side of the dashboard that is visible if the passenger door is open. Either way, set the system and look for proof something changed. Is there a message on the dashboard? Finally, set the system based on the seller's preference in case you do not purchase the car. This is critical.

Emergency Call

This system contacts the emergency services if you crash or activate it via a button. On this basis, it cannot be tested responsibly so check for a warning message that says it is faulty.

Check List 4: Vehicle Inspection

Factor 28: Off Road Use and Aids

Consider the Supporting Material that follows, then note anything that suggests extreme and/or extensive off road use. Also check any special off road features.

....
....
....
....
....
....
....
....
....
....
....
....
....
....
....
....
....
....
....
....
....
....
....
....
....
....
....
....
....
....

Check List 4: Vehicle Inspection

Factor 28: Off Road Use and Aids

Supporting Material

Underbody Protection Plates

Underbody protection plates reinforce key components that might otherwise be wrecked by vicious, off road hazards. The bottom of the engine, for example. The vehicle might have standard, factory fitted plates so their presence alone does not prove it went off road. However, look for anything after market. Nobody adds protection plates then only goes to the supermarket. The vehicle's sales brochure confirms its original specification and is likely available online. Now consider the condition of the plates irrespective of when they were installed. Why? Because if the vehicle has protection it probably has high ground clearance too. Clearly, therefore, there is not much risk of hitting the plates on tarmac roads so a lot of dents, bends, and scuffs suggest more extreme usage.

Terrain Optimiser

This system adjusts the response of various components to suit the terrain. The throttle and transmission, for example. Expect modes such as snow, sand, and rock. Clearly, you cannot test it properly unless you have a wide range of extreme terrain. In addition, there might not be enough time for you to learn to spot the vehicle's subtle changes of behaviour. There is some hope, though. Select a mode then look for proof it engaged. Is there a light on the button? Is there a message on the dashboard? Can you feel a difference, in fact? Also look for a message that says the system is faulty.

Hill Decent Control

Hill decent control regulates the throttle and brakes to

automatically maintain a slow, consistent speed on extreme off road descents. You can test it on tarmac, too. Simply:

- climb to the top of a very steep hill
- engage the system
- accelerate slightly
- release the throttle pedal
- cover the brakes in case the system is faulty
- ensure the car does not exceed about 5 miles per hour.

Check List 4: Vehicle Inspection

Factor 29: Extras for a Convertible

Consider the Supporting Material that follows, then check any features only found in a convertible and list any issues.

Check List 4: Vehicle Inspection

Factor 29: Extras for a Convertible

Supporting Material

Manual Convertible Roof

If the roof retracts manually it is probably made from fabric rather than metal. Look for tears, discolouration, and mould that spoil its look. Further check for engrained dirt that is difficult to remove. Also ensure that the roof retracts without complaint. Do its clamps release? Does it move back smoothly as far as the manufacturer intends? Can it now be closed?

Electric Convertible Roof

See Manual Convertible Roof. In contrast, ensure the roof opens and closes electrically without jamming or struggling. In addition, if there is a problem it might leak hydraulic fluid in the car, on the car, and/or next to the car. Can you see fluid?

Wind Deflector

The wind deflector is a removable screen that sits behind the seats to minimise how much noise, wind, and vibration penetrate the cabin. Consider first how it looks. Is it torn? Confirm too that it folds, bends, and moves as required.

Active Roll Bar

The active roll bar is a safety feature that emerges behind the seats if the car rolls (or is likely to roll). Along with the windscreen, it forms a safety zone to reduce the risk of hitting your head on the road. Proceed with caution if you see it deployed. Something made it deploy. Furthermore, as the bar cannot be tested look for a message that says there is a fault.

Check List 4: Vehicle Inspection

Factor 30: Secondary Security Systems

Consider the Supporting Material that follows, then check the secondary security systems and list any faults.

Check List 4: Vehicle Inspection

Factor 30: Secondary Security Systems

Supporting Material

Alarm

The alarm makes a noise that attracts attention if someone tries to steal the vehicle. There are a couple of points to consider. Although counter intuitive, the first is whether the alarm remains silent when the vehicle is left alone. When nobody tries to steal it, in other words. Why? Because if it is faulty it might go off without a justifiable reason. This is a common problem and particularly annoying at night. I know from experience. So do my neighbours! To evaluate the alarm:

- close the doors, windows, and tailgate
- check the bonnet and fuel flap are shut
- switch the engine off
- lock the vehicle
- do not touch the vehicle
- wait as long as practical
- confirm the alarm stays silent.

The next issue is whether the alarm sounds if required. This might be tricky to test. Perhaps the alarm incorporates a tilt sensor in case someone tries to tow the car. In contrast, perhaps a voltage sensor notes odd power drains on the battery. Forcing a door open turns on the interior lights, for example. That is a power drain. You cannot realistically trigger a tilt or voltage sensor. However, maybe the alarm has internal sensors you can provoke. If so sit in the cabin, set the alarm, and furiously wave your arms. Does the alarm sound? To stop the noise, start the car or press a button on its key fob.

Immobiliser

Without the immobiliser, thieves can easily manipulate the car's ignition wires to make it start without its key fob. On this basis, for example, the immobiliser must receive a deactivation code from the fob before it lets the engine have fuel. Clearly, you cannot test this capability without simulating a crime. Best not! In contrast, you can check the other side of the coin, i.e. that the immobiliser deactivates as required. Note then whether it is tricky to start the car. If it is, look for a warning light that implies the immobiliser is intervening. If lit, maybe there is a fault with the immobiliser or the fob is struggling to transit a code. Try the spare fob to reveal which.

Check List 4: Vehicle Inspection

Factor 31: Entertainment and Connections

Consider the Supporting Material that follows, then note any faults with the entertainment systems and connections.

Check List 4: Vehicle Inspection

Factor 31: Entertainment and Connections

Supporting Material

Stereo Code

Confirm via the car's manual or the internet whether the stereo requires a code to function. The purpose of a code is to electronically link the stereo to the vehicle so thieves cannot remove it, transfer it, and expect it to just work. The problem is that the code can vanish if the battery that helps start the engine goes flat (or is removed). So, look for a message such as 'enter code'. In addition, ensure that the code is recorded elsewhere for the future. Did you see it among the paperwork? If the code is missing the manufacturer might retrieve it for a fee.

Analogue Radio

Analogue radio lets you listen to broadcasts via traditional frequencies. To test it, tune to a station that typically comes through clearly in your part of the world. Now listen. Excess crackling, whistling, and cutting out implies the radio is struggling for a signal. Maybe there is a loose connection. If there is cause for concern, repeat the test via another station before deciding there is a fault. Now test the radio's secondary features. Is the screen clear? Do the volume buttons work?

Now inspect the aerial. If the vehicle is relatively modern, it might have a short, static, rubber aerial on the roof. Is it dry, cracked, and/or rotten? Alternatively, the aerial might be housed within plastic trim that vaguely resembles a shark fin. Is the trim securely attached to the roof? In contrast, if the car is old a telescopic aerial might emerge manually or via an electric motor. If the latter, ensure it pops up automatically as you turn on the radio. If not, perhaps the motor is broken.

Digital Radio

See Analogue Radio for the test procedure. In contrast, digital radio lets you listen via newer, theoretically clearer digital frequencies. However, the station behaves differently if the reception is poor. It is more likely to vanish than come through faintly alongside a lot of cracks and whistles. It is more on/off.

Cassette Player

Oh dear! It seems the car has a cassette player. That is bad news. Why? Because it might inspire you to dig out your old tapes and listen to horrendous eighties pop music. Do you want your passengers' ears to bleed? To test the player, insert an undamaged tape and ensure it is not chewed up as you hit play. Now consider the playback speed. If it is too slow perhaps the drive belt is slipping. Also check the player's secondary features such as pause, rewind, and automatic side swap.

Compact Disc Player (CD)

The player stows a single audio disc. To test it, find a disc that is clean and undamaged. No scratches, please. Does the player accept this disc? Does it play nicely or skip? Also test secondary features such as stop, rewind, and eject. Also check the screen is intact and clear. Look for flickering, for example.

Compact Disc Changer

See Compact Disc Player for the test procedure. In addition, the changer simultaneously stows several discs and lives in the dashboard, boot, or under a seat. Best therefore load a full complement of discs then swap between them. Go 1, 2, 3, for example. Does each disc move to the play position as needed?

Television

In the United Kingdom, the television is redundant if it only receives analogue broadcasts. These days no analogue signal is sent. In contrast, if the set is digital ensure the picture appears. If not, you might have to retune. Confirm too that the programme comes through clearly if there is good reception in your area. Note, however, that the picture might vanish if the screen faces the driver's seat and the car starts to move. This is to encourage you to watch the road instead. You might still hear the audio. Further ensure the screen is intact and the set's secondary features work well. Is there a remote control?

Digital Video Disc Player (DVD)

This player stows a single video disc. The screen is likely built into a front headrest and facing the rear passengers. Grab a clean, undamaged disc to start the test. Does it play without complaint? Note freezing, for example. Now check the player's screen. Is it intact? Also test secondary features such as rewind.

Auxiliary Port (AUX)

Connect your smartphone via this port then play songs stored within it through the vehicle's larger, better quality speakers. Systems vary but the representative test procedure is:

- connect via a 3.5 to 3.5 millimetre cable
- set the vehicle's stereo to auxiliary
- ensure the volume on the stereo is appropriate
- make the volume on the device loud
- find a song via the phone and press play
- confirm the song plays through the car's speakers.

Universal Serial Bus Port (USB)

See Auxiliary Port for the initial insight but connect via a universal serial bus cable. The representative test process is:

- connect the vehicle and device via the cable

- look at the car's screen to see what songs are available
- hit play on a favoured song via the car's interface
- ensure the song plays through the vehicle's speakers.

Bluetooth

Bluetooth lets you connect devices such as a phone without a cable. Calls and music can then be heard via the vehicle's speakers. Systems vary, but a representative test procedure is:

- switch Bluetooth on within the phone
- make the phone visible to compatible devices
- switch on the vehicle's Bluetooth
- find a list of nearby devices via the phone
- connect to the vehicle
- ask a friend to phone you to check all is well.

Steering Wheel Audio Controls

Steering wheel audio controls put various functions at your fingertips, so pick a button to test first. Confirm now that it performs the correct task. Ensure volume up does not change the radio station, for example. Such a fault implies there is an electrical issue. Move now from button to button and repeat.

Wireless Phone Charger

This system charges your phone without a wire. To test it, find a mat in the cabin that incorporates a picture of a phone. Now put your modern, compatible smartphone on the mat. Is it charging? Check the charge indicator for confirmation. There might also be a symbol on the vehicle's dashboard. If the phone does not charge turn it around and try again. It has to sit in a certain position.

Speakers

Even the best stereo cannot compensate for bad speakers, so test them carefully. To get started, centralise the front to rear fade balance. Do the same for the left to right balance. This ensures every speaker is on which is important. Maybe someone switched off – or turned down – the rear speakers so a child could sleep. In addition, set the graphic equalisers to their central positions so the sound is not artificially distorted.

Furthermore, play a song via a high quality recorded format. A compact disc is perfect. It is preferable to the radio as it eliminates any risk of bad reception distorting the test. Now pick a speaker to check first. Does sound emerge? Is the sound acceptable? Any rattle, distortion, or lack of range suggests the speaker is unremarkable. Finally, go from speaker to speaker and repeat the process.

Check List 4: Vehicle Inspection

Factor 32: Water Ingress

Consider the Supporting Material that follows, then list any evidence that suggests the car lets in water.

Check List 4: Vehicle Inspection

Factor 32: Water Ingress

Supporting Material

Life is unpleasant if your vehicle lets in water. Perhaps the seats get soaked. Perhaps your luggage floats around in the boot. Water can cause mould, too. Mould is bad for your health and it smells worse than speciality tea. Water also makes the car corrode. Hello rust and wrecked circuit boards. In addition, finding where water gets in can be tricky as it travels easily. It might pool a long way from the point of entry.

In contrast, perhaps the car is soaked even though it is watertight to the extent intended by the manufacturer. Perhaps a river broke its banks and somebody tried to pass the flooded road adjacent. If so, the damage might be everything mentioned above and far, far more. Consider the engine, for starters. Maybe water got sucked through its air intake and into the cylinders. Perhaps the pressure in the cylinders then got too high. If so, the rods that connect the pistons to the crankshaft might be bent. Any such problem is very serious. The vehicle might be beyond economical repair.

To check for issues, look first for water in areas it might pool such as the spare wheel well in the boot, cup holders, and pockets in the door cards. Now inspect the driver's seat. Are there brown or yellow stains? Can you see mould? Can you smell mould? Touch the fabric, too. Is it damp? Apply the same criteria to the:

- other seats
- cabin carpet
- mats
- boot carpet
- headliner (also check it is not saggy)

That said, be careful not to jump to conclusions and wrongly condemn the vehicle. Note that:

- material can feel damp when it is merely cold
- condensation is inevitable in certain weather
- stains can be caused by a spilt drink.

Check List 4: Vehicle Inspection

Factor 33: Dashboard, Centre Console, and Door Cards

Consider the Supporting Material that follows then check the dashboard, centre console, and door cards and list any defects.

....

....

....

....

....

....

....

....

....

....

....

....

....

....

....

....

....

....

....

....

....

....

....

....

....

....

....

....

Check List 4: Vehicle Inspection

Factor 33: Dashboard, Centre Console, and Door Cards

Supporting Material

The dashboard dominates the cabin so faults are prominent and in your line of sight. Consider first whether it is cracked. Perhaps it spent too long in the sun. Also note scratches, scuffs, and holes for a mobile phone mount. In addition, the dashboard likely has cubbyholes so check each in turn. Does, for instance, the glovebox open properly or does it collapse because the hinge is wrecked? Does it close? Does the lock work? Is the interior damaged? Repeat these checks for the centre console that runs between the front seats and the door cards. The cards are the decorative panels on the inside of the doors. Finally, check any parts in close proximity. For example:

- steering wheel, e.g. note heavy wear
- instrument cluster, e.g. look for cracks
- buttons, e.g. see if any are missing
- badges, e.g. check for damage.

Check List 4: Vehicle Inspection

Factor 34: Boot Fittings

Consider the Supporting Material that follows, then evaluate the boot fittings and jot down any concerns.

Check List 4: Vehicle Inspection

Factor 34: Boot Fittings

Supporting Material

Retractable Load Cover

This cover works like a horizontal roller blind for a window and conceals luggage in the boot. Ensure first that it is present. Perhaps it was removed to increase capacity then misplaced. Confirm too that it is secure while extended. If not, it might spring back at speed and terrify your rear passengers. Also check for damage such as tears, frays, and stains. Now release the cover from the mechanism that keeps it extended. Does it retract easily?

Parcel Shelf

The parcel shelf covers cargo in the boot and rises and falls automatically with the tailgate. Confirm it is present and in satisfactory condition. Note splits, for example. Furthermore, ensure it moves as required. If not, the cord that connects it to the tailgate might be broken or missing. In contrast, there might be an issue with the pivot points at the rear of the shelf.

Variable Height Boot Floor

The variable floor lets you split the cargo bay into horizontal sections. To test it, ensure the panel is present and in good condition. Note stains, for example. Now move it from spot to spot and check it feels solid. Perhaps lean on it a little. Why? Because the manufacturer might specify a weight limit for some positions. If such advice was ignored the floor might be weakened.

Check List 4: Vehicle Inspection

Factor 35: Modifications

Consider the Supporting Material that follows, then list any modifications fitted to the car. Also note the implications.

Check List 4: Vehicle Inspection

Factor 35: Modifications

Supporting Material

Note that the car might be modified, i.e. change of specification since it left the factory. Such work has implications it is important to consider. For starters, in the United Kingdom your insurance company has to be told. The premium might then increase accordingly. If you do not tell the insurer your policy might be invalid. There is then no payout if you have a collision, theft, or other mishap. Also, there might be mechanical problems if modifications have been poorly implemented. For example, I know a car that has:

- engine performance upgrades that make it cut out
- wheel arches that rip the extra wide tyres
- low suspension that makes it hit speed bumps.

On this basis, consider whether anything in the engine bay looks modified. Note that the overall impression was probably plain when the car was new. Are there now parts that look fancy and out of place? Note suspiciously vibrant colours, for example. If necessary, find pictures on the internet that show what the engine bay looks like in factory form. Now look throughout the vehicle for other modifications. Best check the:

- wheel size, e.g. enlarged
- suspension, e.g. lowered
- trim, e.g. carbon fibre added
- lights, e.g. added beneath
- body kit, e.g. bumpers replaced.

Finally, think back to Check List 3. Did you see any invoices among the paperwork that prove the vehicle is modified?

Check List 4: Vehicle Inspection

Factor 36: Miscellaneous

Consider the Supporting Material that follows, then check any miscellaneous systems and list any defects.

Check List 4: Vehicle Inspection

Factor 36: Miscellaneous

Supporting Material

Satellite Navigation

Satellite navigation confirms how to get from the vehicle's current location to your destination. Consider first how the map is stored. Perhaps it is on a memory chip that is permanently integrated into the car. Skip to the next paragraph if this is your scenario. In contrast, maybe it is stored on digital video disc or secure digital card. If so, the player is likely in the dashboard, under a seat, or in the centre console. Whether disc or card, remove it to prove it is present rather than for sale at a popular online auction site. Also check it is a branded, manufacturer supplied original rather than a pirate copy that infringes copyright and might not work reliably.

Now pick a destination such as a local, tricky to find, residential street that is within a couple of miles. Does the system calculate a route? While en route, listen and watch for instructions such as turn left. If there is no instruction, the system might be struggling to get a signal from the satellites. Ensure this is a short term hassle not the typical scenario.

Virtual Cockpit

The virtual cockpit is a computer screen that replaces the traditional instrument cluster. It incorporates the speedometer, for example. To test it, recognise that the cockpit might reboot if it is faulty. The instruments then vanish which is unsettling. Watch for this behaviour. Furthermore, the cockpit lets you choose what information is shown. Move through the options to confirm the buttons, screen, and software work. Check also that your screen is intact and clear.

Head-up Display

Head-up display projects information onto the windscreen such as the car's speed. Note that it likely requires a special windscreen for the image to be clear. Is it clear? If not, perhaps the windscreen broke and the replacement is inferior. If, however, the image is tricky to see adjust the brightness settings before assuming there is a fault. Sunglasses can also make it difficult to see. Furthermore, recognise that the image might initially be incomplete. Perhaps the left half is missing. The likely solution is to optimise its position to suit your line of sight. In contrast, the projection might be on a panel that comes out the dashboard as needed. Does the panel emerge?

Handling Control System

The handling system optimises the behaviour of the car to suit your preferences and/or the conditions. Perhaps you favour a comfortable feel rather than sporty, for example. If the car has a straightforward, old fashioned system it likely relates to a single component. Perhaps you can set the automatic transmission to comfort or sport. However, if the system is advanced there is a wider choice. Choose perhaps comfort, sport, or sport plus to simultaneously adjust the response of the:

- transmission
- suspension
- steering
- throttle
- traction control.

To test the system, check via the car's manual or the internet which components it relates too. Perhaps it is the automatic transmission, steering, and suspension. Now engage the most comfortable mode, drive a couple of miles, and consider how the vehicle behaves. Does the transmission move up its gears at moderate engine revolutions to minimise noise? Is the steering light to make manoeuvres less physically demanding? Is the suspension reasonably soft to make the ride comfortable? Now:

- switch to the sportiest mode
- drive the same route.

Now consider again how the car feels. Does the transmission move up its gears at higher engine revolutions to improve acceleration? Is the steering heavier and more precise? Is the suspension firmer to keep your vehicle flatter through quick, sharp corners? If you cannot feel a difference, the system is faulty or your lack of familiarity makes it tricky to spot the changes. If the former, there might be a message on the dashboard.

Traffic Sign Assist

As you pass a traffic sign this system sees it via a camera. A pictorial representation - not a photograph - then appears on the dashboard. To test it, pass a standard sign that is not obscured by plants, traffic, or an over enthusiastic group of morris dancers. Do you see a representation of the correct sign?

Voice Recognition

This system lets you operate the car's equipment by voice command. Say turn on radio, for example. However, note that it might struggle to interpret some accents and phrases. To check it:

- find a list of commands via the car's manual or the internet
- close the doors and windows so the cabin is quiet
- ask any passengers to stop talking
- press the speak button on the steering wheel

- make the command of your choice (speak clearly)
- ensure the command is implemented.

Fatigue Monitor

This system monitors your behaviour then recommends rest as required. Possible triggers include poor lane discipline, a lack of steering, and sleepy eye movements. Clearly, it is too dangerous to deliberately trigger the monitor but it might come to life on its own if you happen to be tired. Any such warning suggests it works.

Trip Computer

The trip computer reveals various facts about the vehicle. Its average speed, for example. Find the readout to start your test. It might come via a small screen in the instrument cluster that has traditional, pixel style letters and numbers. If so, check the image is complete as pixels vanish with age. Alternatively, there is a big screen that performs numerous tasks. Is the screen intact? Is the picture sharp? Wherever the readout, run through the trip's functions to check the interface works.

Furthermore, note the car's average speed relative to fuel consumption. Why? Because the brochure says it covers a certain number of miles per gallon. For example, 30 in town and 50 on faster roads (40 average). This information might be useful. It might suggest whether the car worked efficiently in the recent past or how it was driven. Maybe the average speed was 22 miles per hour. That indicates town driving. Did the car therefore manage 30 miles per gallon? In contrast, if the average speed was 60 did it do 50 miles per gallon? Naturally, make some allowance in case the manufacturer's figures are optimistic. However, if fuel consumption was poor there might be cause for concern. Potential scenarios include:

- engine not working at peak efficiency

- brake calliper struggling to release
- someone drove the vehicle very hard.

Gear Shift Indicator

This system helps you optimise your driving to minimise fuel consumption. How? By recommending when to change gear. To test it, engage second then accelerate until third is required. Stay in second, though. Now look for a message that tells you to change gear. Follow any suggestion then confirm the system stops nagging.

Router

The router creates a wi-fi network to connect smartphones, laptops, and tablets to the internet. To test it, recognise that a subscription likely has to be paid for the router to work. If it has:

- switch the router on
- scan for the network via your device
- ensure your device connects
- check the connection is stable
- consider whether the connection is fairly fast.

12 Volt Power Socket

Among other things, this socket powers a cigarette lighter or charges your phone. Find it in the dashboard, centre console, or boot. Now:

- connect your smartphone via a suitable cable
- ensure the charge indicator on the phone comes to life.

Horn

If there is danger in close proximity the horn helps you warn other motorists. However, it might come to life of its own volition if there is a fault. Listen for this behaviour throughout the test drive. Furthermore, press the relevant button to confirm the horn sounds when you need it. Is it loud and clear?

Fuel Filler Flap and Cap

The car has a flap in its bodywork that covers the fuel filler cap. Best confirm the flap opens. If not, you cannot refuel and that is a problem. Now remove the cap and inspect its rubber seal. Is it split? If the seal is poor, the vehicle might smell of fuel and the check engine light might come on. Now replace the cap, confirm it tightens, and ensure the flap closes.

Check List 4: Vehicle Inspection

Factor 37: Third Party Inspection

Consider the Supporting Material that follows then decide whether to have the vehicle inspected by an independent, third party mechanic. List any reported faults of note in the space provided.

Check List 4: Vehicle Inspection

Factor 37: Third Party Inspection

Supporting Material

Consider whether to have the car inspected by an independent, third party mechanic. Why bother? Because he/she might confirm your conclusions and provide further valuable insight. This information makes it easier to decide whether to purchase the vehicle. The inevitable penalty is up front cost. However, the investment might be recouped several times over if the mechanic spots a serious, expensive fault that you missed. Whether it is worth the expense depends on the circumstances. The Influencing factors include:

- value of the vehicle
- cost of the inspection
- your confidence the vehicle is sound (or not)
- time constraints
- whether the seller permits such inspection.

Check List 4: Vehicle Inspection

Conclusion

Check List 4 is complete. Get whisky to celebrate. Once sober, review any comments you noted above and decide whether you want to buy the car. Go home if it has too many niggles. Go home faster if it has a major flaw that is unacceptable. In contrast, if the vehicle is satisfactory continue to Check List 5.

Check List 5:

Make the Deal

Check List 5: Make the Deal

Contents

Check List 5 enables you to confidently, politely, and calmly negotiate tremendous terms of sale. It incorporates:

- Factor 1: Valuation
- Factor 2: Trade-in
- Factor 3: Negotiation
- Factor 4: Collection

Check List 5: Make the Deal

Factor 1: Valuation

Consider the Supporting Material that follows, then note the vehicle's fair market value in the space provided.

Check List 5: Make the Deal

Factor 1: Valuation

Supporting Material

To buy with confidence you must personally confirm the car's fair market value. You cannot assume the seller priced it correctly. Get a valuation from a credible and independent online guide. Independent is the key term. On this basis, pick a supplier that has no vested interest in the vehicle or its valuation. Ensure there is no reason to value it too low, in other words. A low valuation is more probable if your supplier:

- assumes you already own the car
- is simultaneously offering to buy it.

Furthermore, ensure the valuation is as specific as possible to the vehicle and its circumstance. The relevant factors include:

- make
- model
- power source, e.g. 2.0 litre engine
- fuel type, e.g. petrol
- transmission, e.g. manual
- trim, e.g. LX
- year of registration, e.g. 2019
- registration age identifier, e.g. 19
- mileage, e.g. 10,206
- type of seller, e.g. franchise
- condition, e.g. excellent
- optional extras, e.g. satellite navigation.

Perhaps the valuation is £10,000. Fine. That is a helpful starting point. However, there are multiple guides and each has its own perspective so cross reference the valuation. Also, note how much people are asking for similar cars. In other words, trawl through the classifieds. Rather, therefore, than conclude your vehicle is worth exactly £10,000 establish a range based on several resources. £9,750 to £10,250, maybe.

In addition, compare the range to the seller's asking price. You might conclude the seller wants 20 percent above market value. Perhaps he/she is greedy, misinformed, or an optimist. Whatever the reason, any negotiated discount is unlikely to match such a percentage. Are you willing to overpay? You might be if you love the car. In contrast, perhaps the seller's price is suspiciously low. That is either an opportunity to save money or a warning that something is wrong. Having tested the vehicle, inspected its paperwork, and met the seller which do you think is most probable? The possible scenarios include:

- car has a serious fault that is expensive to repair
- professional trader is very keen to hit a sales target
- private seller is emigrating so needs a fast transaction
- seller is struggling to find a buyer.

Check List 5: Make the Deal

Factor 2: Trade-in

Consider the Supporting Material that follows, then decide whether to trade-in your current car or dispose of it independently. Pick from:

- trade-in
- dispose independently.

Check List 5: Make the Deal

Factor 2: Trade-in

Supporting Material

Do you own a vehicle that is no longer required? Are you also buying its replacement from a dealership? If so, consider whether to trade it in as part payment. The alternative is to sell it separately. Either way, confirm its value via independent guides. Naturally, there are pros and cons however you dispose of your unwanted car. The benefits of trade-in include:

- immediate disposal
- no advertising costs
- potential buyers cannot visit your home
- less risk of uninsured test drives
- reduced risk of a fraudulent payment
- no need to simultaneously insure, tax, and maintain both cars.

Possible disadvantages include:

- lower price than if you sell privately, but any difference might be offset against the aforementioned savings
- car might be scrapped prematurely if it is worth more as parts.

Check List 5: Make the Deal

Factor 3: Negotiation

Consider the Supporting Material that follows, then note your negotiating baseline in the space provided.

Check List 5: Make the Deal

Factor 3: Negotiation

Supporting Material

Negotiation is not as frightening as you might think. It is simply your opportunity to chat with the seller and agree mutually acceptable terms. That is all there is to it. The stages below reveal the structure of your easy to follow, purely theoretical negotiation at a dealership plus the techniques that help you succeed. Adapt and apply the information to your real negotiation.

Stage 1: Set the Scene

The negotiation starts informally the moment you walk on the forecourt. Why? Because within seconds the seller decides whether to like you, hate you, or something between. You are more likely to be offered better terms if liked so be friendly, smile, and make a little small talk. Treat the seller like a respected colleague rather than your nemesis. There is no nemesis. You are simply talking to another person about the car. It is no big deal.

Furthermore, recognise that the seller is not going to negotiate unless there is a realistic chance of a sale. Why bother otherwise? On this basis, explain that you are ready to buy the moment someone offers you the right vehicle and terms. This encourages the seller to take you seriously rather than perceive you as a time waster. There are plenty of time wasters. However, this statement is not a promise to buy. You can still walk away.

For balance, never appear too keen. Never suggest that your current car is wrecked and you need a replacement today, for example. Such comments prove you are in a weak negotiating position. Why would the seller now offer you the best possible terms? You are clearly desperate for transport so cannot be too choosy, take your time, or dither. Keep such problems to yourself.

Stage 2: Recognise Incentives

Recognise too that negotiation is merely the exchange of incentives. An incentive is anything that has a value to you and/or the seller. On this basis, the seller wants you to buy the vehicle so offers incentives that make it more likely. Good! That is completely legitimate and in your favour. You might be offered:

- money, e.g. price lowered
- MOT, e.g. safety inspection
- warranty, e.g. insurance that covers the cost of repair
- service, e.g. maintenance
- repairs, e.g. scratch removal
- consumables, e.g. wiper blades, tyres, fuel
- accessories, e.g. floor mats, boot liner, fluffy dice
- valeting, e.g. professional clean
- trade-in, i.e. accepts your current car as part payment.

In addition, recognise that you want to purchase the car but cannot without the seller's permission and cooperation. You therefore have to convince the seller to hand over the key. In other words, you have to exchange incentives not just receive them. There is no deal unless the seller is happy, too. It is important to remember that. Incentives you might exchange include:

- cash injection, e.g. to purchase new stock
- maximise profit, e.g. the longer the car sits on the forecourt the less it is worth
- cut costs, e.g. no need to continue to pay for advertising

- success, e.g. hit the end of month sales target
- space, e.g. remove the car from the forecourt
- loss of responsibility, e.g. no longer the seller's problem if the vehicle is stolen, vandalised, or develops a fault
- opportunity, e.g. trade-in can be sold for further profit.

Stage 3: Define Your Baseline

Stage 3 invites you to define a baseline. The baseline is your least favoured – yet still acceptable – terms. In other words, what must the seller offer as a minimum for you to purchase the car? The baseline provides clarity of thought, helps you negotiate with confidence, and eliminates any risk of stumbling into a bad deal. If the seller meets or exceeds your baseline there is every reason to buy the car. If the seller cannot meet your baseline simply go home. Your baseline is:

- money: £9,850
- MOT: 12 months
- warranty: 3 months
- service: free minor
- repairs: none
- consumables: free front tyres
- accessories: none
- valeting: none
- trade-in: none.

Check List 3, 4, and 5 enabled you to define the aforementioned baseline. Your work confirmed the vehicle needs a service, for example. Furthermore, note that the baseline is realistic rather than greedy, fanciful, and unfair. The seller is not going to halve the asking price, fix every minor imperfection, then pop over to your house to mow the lawn. Such unrealistic expectations:

- make you look foolish

- irritate the seller
- suggest you are a time waster
- make the seller less likely to negotiate.

Stage 4: Seller's First Offer

Recognise now that the seller makes the first offer of the negotiation by default. Why? Because the car's advert that is available online specifies the terms. The seller's first offer is:

- money: £10,000
- MOT: 12 months
- warranty: 3 months
- service: none
- repairs: none
- consumables: none
- accessories: none
- valeting: none
- trade-in: none.

The seller's first offer is rather interesting. Recognise that some of the terms already satisfy your baseline. Others fall short. The terms that must be improved via the negotiation are:

- money: £10,000 (baseline says you can only pay £9,850)
- service: none (baseline says you need a free minor service)
- consumables: none (baseline says you want free front tyres).

Stage 5: Your First Offer

Now is the time to make your first offer. Naturally, ensure it is inspired by the terms the seller must improve to hit your baseline. However, remember that the baseline defines your least favoured acceptable terms not the optimum – so ask for more. Asking for more also gives you the opportunity to later adjust your terms if needed without falling short of the baseline. Furthermore, specify every term within your offer to ensure the seller understands it. Be clear and concise. This is not the time to be vague, timid, and wordy. Your first offer is:

- money: £9,650 (better than your baseline that says you can pay up to £9,850)
- MOT: 12 months (meets baseline)
- warranty: 3 months (meets baseline)
- service: free major (better than your baseline that says you only need a free minor service)
- repairs: free bumper repair (better than your baseline that proves it is not essential to have the bumper fixed)
- consumables: free front tyres (meets baseline)
- accessories: none (meets baseline)
- valeting: none (meets baseline)
- trade-in: none (meets baseline).

Stage 6: Seller's Counteroffer

The seller now refuses your offer. Never mind. Stay calm and friendly. Now ask a question that invites a useful reply. Ask what can be done to move the negotiation forward? This encourages the seller to make a counteroffer. From your perspective, the counteroffer is better than the seller's first offer but worse than yours. It is in the middle. On this basis, the seller says you can have the free major service you requested. This is better than your baseline that only requires a free minor service.

Did you see what just happened? Your question encouraged the seller to give you an incentive without receiving anything in return. Excellent! That is as good as it gets at the negotiating table. However, despite the progress some terms within the seller's counteroffer still fall short of your baseline. They are:

- money: £10,000 (baseline says you can only pay £9,850)
- consumables: none (baseline says you need free front tyres).

Stage 7: Your Counteroffer

The next move is to make your own counteroffer to get the free front tyres. However, it is unrealistic to expect the seller to continue to give you incentives without receiving anything in return. As such, offer to pay £9,700 (increased from £9,650) in exchange for tyres. Also offer to forgo the bumper repair. Now brace yourself. Why? Because your counteroffer is flatly rejected.

Stage 8: End the Negotiation

Despite the setback, now is the moment to bring your negotiation to a successful conclusion. The key is to push harder via a respectful, realistic final offer that is also an ultimatum. So:

- promise to purchase the vehicle now with no further negotiation if the seller accepts your forthcoming offer
- confirm this offer is final and cannot be improved
- explain the offer is superior to any previous offer
- offer £9,750 (up from £9,700 but still less than baseline)
- say you still need the free tyres and service, etc.

Also emphasise any additional benefits the seller receives once your offer is accepted. For example, the car will be sold immediately rather than days, weeks, or months later. That is significant as it is losing value. Every day it gets a little older, a little rustier, and a little less desirable to other buyers. It is clearly in the seller's interest to move it on fast.

The seller now has a simple choice. Accept your sensible, immediately available, final offer and sell the car or wait for another buyer. Furthermore, there is no point asking for additional incentives as you said your offer is final. It is therefore accepted. Good. Shake hands and try not to jump for joy.

Stage 9: Get it in Writing

Confirm the final terms of sale in writing. This makes it harder for the seller to later withdraw incentives or have memory problems. Naturally, check the paperwork before you sign and ensure the seller corrects any mistakes, omissions, and/or ambiguities. Take nothing for granted. I once negotiated a deal and the seller wrote 'try to remove a scratch' from the wing. However, I had it changed to 'remove the scratch'. This change was important. The word 'try' gave the seller a chance to:

- improve the scratch rather than remove it
- try to improve the scratch, but fail
- do no work but claim there was a valiant attempt.

Traps and How to Avoid Them

Your real negotiation might not flow as smoothly as the aforementioned example. Perhaps the seller refuses to negotiate. In this scenario, he/she might be genuinely determined not to offer any further incentives. Alternatively, the seller is willing to negotiate but only if you push hard. In other words, he/she is seeing whether you can be easily brushed aside. Many people can. To test the seller's intention:

- stay calm, polite, and friendly

- emphasise that you want to buy the car now
- make a sensible offer
- confirm the offer expires at noon tomorrow
- give the seller your phone number
- move towards the exit.

So what happens now? If the seller is bluffing he/she might backtrack immediately. Excellent. You can now negotiate. In contrast, if there is no movement the seller is genuinely determined to stick to the terms. However, he/she might have a change of heart a few hours later. This is common, so leave on good terms and be ready for a call. It might not come, but this strategy gives you a last chance to buy the car. Why not try?

There are various other traps to consider. Perhaps the seller tries to weaken your negotiating prowess by asking simple, apparently harmless questions that encourage you to answer yes. The only sensible answer is yes, in fact. Maybe these questions also make comparisons with your existing car. For instance, are you pleased the replacement is significantly safer for your children? Are you glad it is more environmentally responsible? Might the accompanying used car warranty save you money long term?

How can you answer no to these questions? Any negative response is clearly daft. On this basis, any positive replies – replies the seller can remind you of later – make it hard to walk away from the car without feeling like an idiot. After all, you admit it is:

- safer for your children than your current vehicle
- more environmentally friendly than your existing car
- backed by a warranty that might save you money.

It is easy to escape this question trap. Say, you know the car has strengths but now is the time to focus on the terms of sale. In other words, there is no need to answer the seller's leading questions. Just brush them off. Best be friendly despite the provocation as you lose credibility the moment you get flustered. Cool, calm, and collected is the best approach by far.

Time can be used against you, too. Maybe the seller says his/her offer includes special terms that expire at the end of the day. Buy today or pay more tomorrow. Alternatively, the seller claims there is somebody else desperate to purchase the vehicle if you cannot commit immediately. Such statements might be true but what is the likelihood? Even if the seller is being honest you can always get another car. Never be rushed. There is never a rush to make a wrong decision.

Also consider flattery. Perhaps the seller claims you look fantastic in the car and it will make your friends jealous. Disregard such nonsense. Who cares what other people think about your car? Are they going to drive it? Are they going to pay? Furthermore, beware if the seller acts like your best friend rather than a new acquaintance. It is harder to say no to a friend.

Finally, the seller might talk to excess about the weather, a holiday, or an embarrassing rash no doctor can cure. But why? Maybe he/she is just chatty and there is no malice. In contrast, perhaps the seller is dominating the conversation to make you feel powerless, confused, and flustered. You are then more likely to make a negotiating error. To counteract, say you would like to chat but time is short and steer the conversation back to the car.

Check List 5: Make the Deal

Factor 4: Collection

Consider the Supporting Material that follows, then list any steps to take before collecting the vehicle.

Check List 5: Make the Deal

Factor 4: Collection

Supporting Material

There are final considerations before you take the car home.

Terms of Sale

Check the vehicle meets the terms of sale. Perhaps the seller promised to fit new tyres, for instance. Does it have new tyres?

New Damage

The car is not immune to damage if it stays with the seller for a few days after the negotiation, so briefly check for new issues. The moment you leave the seller can say you caused any new dents, scratches, and scuffs. How can you prove otherwise?

Paperwork

Clearly, the car's paperwork is important so ensure you take it home. It is too easy to assume the seller left it in the glovebox. That is risky. Consider loosing the service history. The vehicle's value might plummet. And what about any proof of warranty? Such paperwork can be worth its weight in gold.

Trade-in

Perhaps the terms of sale incorporate a trade-in, i.e. your unwanted car passes to the seller as part payment for the replacement. Best prepare for this moment. Possible steps include:

- settle outstanding finance

- remove valuables
- retain personal registration
- put paperwork in the glovebox
- place spare key in the glovebox.

Legal

The vehicle is becoming your legal responsibility so take the necessary steps. In the United Kingdom ensure it has:

- motor insurance
- vehicle excise duty
- MOT (if old enough).

Breakdown Insurance

Breakdown insurance is a sensible investment. It guarantees a mechanic comes to your rescue at the roadside if the vehicle develops a fault. It is unproven long term, after all. This cover:

- provides peace of mind
- minimises expenditure if you have a problem
- reduces downtime.

Driving Home

Consider your state of mind before leaving with the car. If you are too excited, nervous, or flustered you are more likely to make a mistake on the road. So, if necessary, take a moment to catch your breath. Finally:

- check you have enough fuel or battery power
- adjust the seat and set the mirrors
- confirm the location of the primary controls
- note any blind spots.

That is it. Mission accomplished. You have successfully bought a second-hand vehicle. Now you can enjoy it and look forward to many shared adventures. The open road awaits. Have fun!

Appendix

Appendix Contents

This Appendix relates to Check List 1 Factor 5: Equipment. It summarises what equipment your car could have and how it typically functions. It is categorised for easy reference. Expect:

- Doors, Tailgate, Bonnet, and Locks
- Windows
- Mirrors
- Wheels and Tyres
- Lights
- Wipers and Washers
- Brakes
- Steering
- Seats
- Seatbelts
- Heating, Ventilation, and Air Conditioning
- Manoeuvring Aids
- Collision Protection
- Off Road Aids
- Extras for a Convertible
- Secondary Security Systems
- Entertainment and Connections
- Boot Fittings
- Miscellaneous

Doors, Tailgate, Bonnet, and Locks

Soft Close Door System

This system eliminates any need to slam the doors shut. It is useful at night if you want to be quiet. Simply push your door until it is almost flush with the adjacent bodywork. Now watch, wait a moment, and ensure it is automatically pulled closed.

Powered Tailgate

Operates via a motor to minimise physical effort.

Powered Tailgate Limiter

Stops the powered tailgate rising beyond a certain height. You might limit its travel to stop it hitting your garage door.

Kick Tailgate

The kick tailgate opens as you wave your foot beneath the rear bumper. It is handy if your hands are full. To stop unauthorised access, it only works if the key fob is nearby.

Active Bonnet

The active bonnet is a safety feature for pedestrians. If somebody hits the front of the car the bonnet lifts slightly via a spring. It then bounces to cushion the impact and minimise injury.

Manual Locking System

Requires you to operate every lock individually via a traditional key.

Central Locking System

Simultaneously operate multiple locks via a traditional key.

Remote Central Locking System

Work multiple locks simultaneously with a wireless fob. There is therefore no need to find a key slot which is tricky in low light.

Keyless Entry System

Ensures there is no need to interact with the car's key fob to operate the locks. If the fob is in close proximity, press the button on the driver's door handle then every lock opens simultaneously. Tap the button again to relock. Alternatively, you might configure the system to only operate the driver's door lock.

Automatic Locking System

Locks the cabin and tailgate once the car hits a certain speed.

Manual Child Lock System

Stops the rear interior door handles working so kids cannot let themselves out. The exterior handles continue to operate normally.

Electric Child Lock System

See Manual Child Lock System for the overview. In contrast, set both locks simultaneously via a switch by the driver's seat.

Windows

Manual Window System

Requires you to operate every opening window via a handle.

Front Electric Window System

The front side windows move electrically to minimise physical effort. As the driver, you have a master panel that opens and closes both. The front passenger has a single switch that operates his/her window only. Rear windows move manually.

Front and Rear Electric Window System

See Front Electric Window System for the initial insight. In addition, the rear windows move electrically rather than manually.

Electric Window Safety System

Stops the windows closing if they are likely to trap your fingers.

Electric Window Lock System

The electric window lock deactivates the rear switches which is handy if you have children. However, as the driver you can still operate the windows from the master control panel.

Heated Windscreen

The heated windscreen removes frost and condensation via thin, barely visible, heated wires within. Visibility is then improved.

Rear Window Demist

See Heated Windscreen for the overview.

Permanent Privacy Glass

This dark tint is permanently integrated into the glass. It provides privacy, makes it hard for thieves to see valuables, and partly blocks the sun. It also makes it harder to see out at night.

Manual Sunroof

The sunroof is a tinted window in the forward section of the vehicle’s roof. Its purpose is to let light and air penetrate the cabin. For the latter, it lifts at its rear edge and can additionally slide out of sight into the roof. Movement is manual.

Electric Sunroof

See Manual Sunroof for the overview but it moves electrically.

Panoramic Roof

See Manual Sunroof and Electric Sunroof for the overview. In contrast, the panoramic roof is larger and it extends over the rear passengers. Its additional purpose is to give everyone a good view of the outside so they can admire scenery. It is great if you want to look up at a mountain range, for example.

Mirrors

Manual Door Mirror Adjustment System

Requires you to move the mirrors to the favoured spots via small, internal wands.

Electric Door Mirror Adjustment System

Lets you adjust both mirrors electrically from the driver's seat.

Heated Exterior Mirror System

Removes frost and condensation from the exterior mirrors.

Manual Fold Door Mirror System

Fold the door mirrors flatter against the sides of the car to reduce its width (while parked). There is then less chance of them being hit by passing cars. The mirrors have to be moved by hand.

Electric Fold Door Mirror System

See Manual Fold Door Mirror System for the initial insight. In contrast, the mirrors operate electrically and simultaneously.

Electric Rear-view Mirror

Move the rear-view mirror to the favoured spot via a motor.

Dimming Rear-view Mirror

Mirror darkens when it might otherwise reflect light from the following vehicle into your eyes. It adds more tint, in other words. The mirror then gets lighter as required. If the troubling car overtakes, for example. The traditional alternative is to flick a lever that points the mirror towards the roof of your car.

Vanity Mirror

Do you want to comb your hair, adjust your clothes, and remove remnants of lunch from between your teeth? If so, the vanity mirror that sits in your sun visor comes to the rescue.

Wheels and Tyres

Steel Wheel Set

The steel wheel set has a utilitarian look that is not particularly attractive. Each wheel therefore has a removable, decorative, plastic hubcap to make it look smart. Scuffing a kerb might wreck the hubcaps but they can be replaced for a modest sum.

Alloy Wheel Set

The alloy set looks smarter than its steel counterpart. The

wheels therefore have a high quality, smart, and stylish look so there is no need for hubcaps (unlike the steel set). There is a downside. If you scuff the wheels on a kerb you have to have them refurbished rather than replace hubcaps. Refurbishment is costly.

Locking Wheel Nut System

This system makes it hard for criminals to steal your wheels and tyres. It incorporates a single locking nut for each wheel that can only be undone via an adaptor. A wrench alone is insufficient.

Tyre Pressure Monitor System

Warns you that a tyre is short of air.

Puncture Repair Kit

The repair kit is the smaller, lighter alternative to a spare tyre. It contains an electric pump and a can of sealant. The pump forces sealant into the tyre to fill the hole. However, it cannot fill larger holes. The electric pump can also reinflate your tyre.

Lights

Halogen Headlamp System

Incorporates traditional low cost bulbs.

Xenon Headlamp System

Brighter, whiter, longer lasting bulbs than the halogen system.

Bi-xenon Headlamp System

Each headlamp has a single bulb that produces the standard and main beam. More traditional lamps have separate bulbs. On this basis, shutters partly cover the bulbs when less light is required. They retract when you switch on the main beams.

Daytime Running Light System

This system ensures the car is always lit to reduce the risk of collision. It is not supposed to help you see, though. It is to help you be seen. It comes on automatically alongside the engine and/or motor. It goes off as you turn on the headlights.

Static Cornering Light System

Improves visibility while cornering. Turn left, for example, then an extra light springs to life on that side of the car to illuminate the corner. It turns off once your turn is complete.

Active Corning Light System

Front lights turn with the steering to better illuminate the road.

Follow Me Home Light System

Ensures some of the exterior lights stay lit once the car is parked and turned off. Why? To illuminate the route to your front door, shed, or that secret pile of cash buried in the garden. The system switches off automatically after a few seconds.

Smart High Beam System

Maximises visibility and minimises the risk of dazzling other motorists. As such, if a car comes towards you at night the system automatically swaps from main to standard beams. As the vehicle passes, the main beams come back on to optimise your view.

Automatic Headlight System

This feature switches on the headlights once it is dark.

Manual Headlamp Leveller System

The car's headlamps point to the optimum position. Not too high and not too low. As such, if for example the boot is full of heavy cargo the rear suspension compresses more than typical. This simultaneously points the front of the vehicle - and therefore its lamps - higher which might impede your visibility and dazzle other drivers. The manual levelling system lets you simultaneously point the lamps higher or lower as needed.

Automatic Headlamp Leveller System

See Manual Headlamp Leveller System but the process is automated.

Wipers and Washers

Automatic Windscreen Wiping System

The system comes to life once the sensor detects it is raining. The wipers then move at the speed and frequency required, get faster or slower as necessary, and stop once the weather improves.

Headlamp Washer System

Cleans the headlamps with water to improve visibility.

Brakes

Antilock Brake System

Without antilock the car might skid if you brake too hard, i.e. slide with its wheels locked. It cannot be steered properly in this state. Antilock recognises that the wheels are locked - or that they are about to lock - then reduces the brake pressure to help them spin. It also shortens the stopping distance.

Emergency Brake Assist

This system reduces your stopping distance if there is an emergency. It works on the basis that you brake very, very fast in such circumstance - but not hard enough. In other words, you move your foot quickly from the throttle to the brake pedal but press the latter far too lightly. On this basis, the system recognises your fast footwork and increases the brake pressure. There is then risk of hitting the hazard. Phew!

Autonomous Emergency Braking

This feature monitors the distance between the front of your car and hazards. If it becomes short relative to how much space is required to stop, it warns you via an audible tone and a message on the dashboard. If you then fail to react, the system brakes on your behalf to avoid an impact or mitigate its severity.

Adaptive Brake Light System

If you brake hard, this system makes your brake lights flash rather than shine constantly (as is typical). The hazard lights flash, too. Its purpose is to warn following drivers that your vehicle is losing speed faster than the world's most lethargic racehorse. There is then less chance of a rear impact.

Brake Pad Wear Indicator System

Indicates it is time to replace the brake pads.

Electric Parking Brake

In contrast to a traditional parking brake, the electric version can work autonomously. It also takes up less room in the cabin.

Steering

Power Steering

Makes the steering lighter and easier to use. How much lighter is defined by the car's speed. At low speed, a lot of steering is required to squeeze into parking bays. Expect the steering to be at its lightest. In contrast, at motorway speed very little steering is required and the vehicle can feel vague if there is too much power assistance. Expect the steering to be heavier.

Manual Steering Wheel Adjustment

Manually move the steering wheel to a comfortable position that does not block your view of the key instruments, e.g. speedometer.

Electric Steering Wheel Adjustment

See Manual Steering Wheel Adjustment. In contrast, your wheel moves to the favoured position via an electric motor and automatically rises to its highest once you switch the vehicle off. The elevated position ensures there is more space to get out.

Heated Steering Wheel

Stops your fingers begging for mercy on frosty mornings.

Seats

Manual Seat

Seat moves to your favoured position by hand.

Electric Seat

Seat moves to your preferred position electrically.

Memory Seat

Seat remembers preset positions which is handy if the car has several drivers. Each position is allocated a numbered button.

Heated Seat

The seat's back support and cushion get warm to keep you comfortable on cold days. Options are hot, hotter, and overcooked.

Massaging Seat

The massaging seat incorporates air pockets that repeatedly fill and empty to massage your back, hips, and legs.

Ventilated Seat

The ventilated seat incorporates fans that circulate air throughout its surface to keep you cool. It is great on warm days.

Folding Rear Seat System

The vertical back support of the rear bench folds against the horizontal cushion. Why bother? So luggage too large for the boot can stretch into the cabin. The back support folds as a single piece, so there is then no room for rear passengers.

Split and Fold Rear Seat System

See Folding Rear Seat System. However, the back support splits into sections rather than as a single piece. This lets you extend the boot yet leave some of the seats upright for passengers.

Tumbling Seat

The tumbling seat makes it easier to carry cargo. Its vertical back support releases, folds against the horizontal cushion, then the whole lot rolls forward into the floor well to make room behind. Check there is nobody in the seat before you fold it.

Removable Seat

The removable seat detaches from the vehicle to be stowed separately. There is then more room for luggage.

Occasional Third Row Seating System

This seating emerges from the floor of the boot. The penalty is that it then occupies most of the space typically reserved for luggage. In addition, it is tricky to access and not particularly comfortable. This seating best suits small people and short trips.

Active Headrest

If the car crashes, the active headrest moves forward and up to limit how far your head jolts backward. Why? To reduce the risk of whiplash which is a neck injury caused by sudden, sharp movement.

ISOFIX System

ISOFIX is the fast, simple, and convenient way to connect a child seat to your vehicle without relying on an adult seatbelt.

Seatbelts

Seatbelt Reminder System

Beeps if someone forgets to wear a seatbelt.

Seatbelt Pre-tensioner System

The pre-tensioner system removes slack from the seatbelts if the vehicle is likely to crash. Expect a sharp, fast, and somewhat aggressive pull. Removing slack keeps you in the best position to benefit from any further safety systems. The airbags, for example.

Heating, Ventilation, and Air Conditioning

Air Conditioning

Air conditioning lowers the temperature in the cabin to stop you stewing in a pool of sweat. It is more effective than opening the windows. Furthermore, it doubles as a dehumidifier so it helps remove any condensation in the cabin that makes the windows foggy.

Cooled Glovebox

The glovebox incorporates a channel that connects to the air conditioning system. It lets you slightly chill your drink.

Climate Control

Climate control lets you set a temperature preference for the cabin. 21 degrees, for example. It then regulates the air conditioning and heater as required. It therefore eliminates any need to manually switch on the air conditioning if the sun comes out. In contrast, you do not have to turn on the heater if the weather takes a turn for the worse. Just pick a temperature and forget it.

Dual Climate Control

See Climate Control. Furthermore, the dual element adds separate temperature preferences for the driver and front passenger.

Triple Climate Control

See Climate Control and Dual Climate Control for the initial insight. However, expect separate temperature preferences for the:

- driver
- front passenger
- all the rear passengers as a single entity.

Quadruple Climate Control

See Climate Control and Dual Climate Control for the initial insight, but expect individual preferences for the:

- driver
- front passenger
- rear left passenger
- rear right passenger.

Manoeuvring Aids

Cruise Control

Cruise control regulates the throttle to maintain your favoured speed. It is not perfect, though. Why? Because it cannot brake so the vehicle exceeds your preference on steep, downward hills if engine braking cannot overcome the pull of gravity. In addition, you plough on irrespective of any hazards ahead such as slow traffic. You have to cancel cruise control manually or crash.

Cruise Control With Brake Function

See Cruise Control for the overview. In addition, the system brakes to help the car maintain speed on steep, downward hills.

Adaptive Cruise Control

See Cruise Control and Cruise Control With Brake Function. In addition, the adaptive element lets the car fall below your set speed if required. If the traffic ahead is too slow, in other words. Your vehicle accelerates back to your set speed once the road is clear.

Speed Limiter

Lets you specify a speed the car cannot easily exceed. Excess, gentle throttle pressure cannot then push it above what is legal and/or safe for the scenario. Press the throttle hard to override.

Intelligent Speed Limiter

See Speed Limiter for the overview. In addition, the system automatically adjusts the maximum permitted speed to match the legal limit. How? By spotting traffic signs via a camera. Further confirmation comes from the car's satellite navigation as it recognises what road it is on. It therefore knows the legal limit.

Rear Parking Sensor System

This parking system helps you easily judge distance while reversing. It therefore bounces signals off hazards such as walls. Beeps of varying frequency reveal whether the hazard is close, very close, or closer than a shave from the world's best razor.

Front Parking Sensor System

See Rear Parking Sensor System but expect guidance at the front.

Reversing Camera

This feature reveals hazards behind via a camera and colour screen. Furthermore, the picture incorporates lines that show where the car is likely to go if you keep the steering at its existing angle. This guidance helps you line up with parking bays.

Around View Monitor

The monitor provides a bird's eye, 360 degree view of the surroundings to make low speed manoeuvres easy. The images come via a camera on each side of the car and a screen on the dashboard. Expect a picture of the roof and any hazards to the front, rear, left, and right of the car. You can also simultaneously see a large image from any other camera.

Blind Spot Monitor

Blind spot monitor confirms that a nearby, adjacent vehicle approaching from the rear is concealed by part of your car’s bodywork. Its purpose is to stop you cutting across the other vehicle’s path and wrecking your paint. The warning comes via a light in the closest exterior mirror. Expect an audible alarm too.

Park Assist

The system steers automatically into parking spaces while you control the throttle, transmission, and brakes. It steers out too.

Lane Departure Warning

Lane departure warning monitors the position of your vehicle relative to the lane marks via a camera. Expect an alert if it wanders off line. You can then make the correction if required.

Lane Keeping Aid

See Lane Departure Warning for insight. In contrast, the system applies torque (turning force) to the steering to nudge the car back to its optimum line. However, it cannot take full control of the steering so do not expect miracles. Only expect a gentle prod.

Hill Assist

For example, stops the vehicle rolling back if you start on a steep hill and struggle to find the bite point of the clutch.

Traction Control

Engages if any driven tyre struggles for traction as you accelerate. It cuts engine power and/or applies any relevant brake.

Electronic Stability Control

Helps maintain a safe line through corners by reducing engine power and/or braking. It minimises understeer and oversteer, in other words. For instance, the system might intervene if you charge into a corner too fast or steer sharply to avoid a crash.

Rear Cross Traffic Alert

Reversing out a parking space can be tricky if the adjacent vehicles block your view of any traffic approaching from your sides. The traditional solution is to reverse very, very slowly without a good view but this is less fun than algebra. The rear cross alert is the solution as it scans for traffic via the parking sensors. Expect a visual and audible warning as necessary.

Night Vision

Night vision makes it easier to see people and animals in low light. It works via an infrared camera that can distinguish between cool, lifeless objects and warmer living creatures. You see its interpretation via a screen on the dashboard. Darker colours represent lifeless objects such as houses, vehicles, and fence posts. Anything living has a far brighter, contrasting look.

Collision Protection

Driver Airbag

This airbag protects your face, head, and chest if there is a collision. It is normally deflated and concealed in the centre of the steering wheel. However, if needed it expands at high speed and breaks through. If you move forward in your seat, you therefore hit the bag which is softer than the steering wheel. The bag then deflates to make it easier to get out the vehicle. Every airbag in the car works on this premise. See below.

Passenger Airbag

Sits forward of the passenger seat in the dashboard.

Side Airbag System

The system protects the driver and front passenger, so an airbag emerges from the side of each seat at about shoulder height. There is then less risk of being hurt by the doors, windows, and/or any debris that approaches the car from its sides.

Curtain Airbag System

The curtain system protects the driver, front passenger, and outer rear passengers. The airbags sit close to the roof, deploy downwards, and span the length of the cabin on both sides.

Pedestrian Airbag

If a pedestrian strikes the front of the vehicle this airbag emerges from under the bonnet. It then covers part of the windscreen and the adjacent pillars. That is great in such circumstance. However, if the bag is too sensitive it might be triggered by hitting a pothole. Whatever the trigger, resetting the bag can cost a fortune. There are countless horror stories.

Passenger Airbag Deactivation System

If you have a child seat in the front of the vehicle, the passenger airbag might knock it out of its safest position if there is a collision. The occupant might then get hurt. The deactivation switch ensures the airbag stays in the dashboard.

Emergency Call

Contacts the emergency services if the car crashes. It then relays your position in whatever language is appropriate to the region. In addition, you can engage the system manually via a switch if you are first on the scene of someone else's crash.

Off Road Aids

Terrain Optimiser

Optimises the response of various systems to suit the terrain. This minimises the risk of getting stuck. Choose snow mode if the weather is terrible, for example. It softens the response of the throttle to minimise wheel spin. Alternatively, select sand mode if you park on a beach. It makes the automatic transmission more lively. The system also optimises the:

- suspension
- brakes
- traction control
- ride height.

Hill Decent Control

Automatically maintains a slow, constant speed on extreme off road descents to reduce the risk of mishap. All you do is steer.

Underbody Protection Plates

Reinforces key parts such as the bottom of the engine to protect them from off road hazards such as rocks, logs, and uneven ground.

Extras For a Convertible

Manual Convertible Roof

The roof retracts to let the pouring rain, howling wind, and freezing snow enter your otherwise comfortable cabin. It also moves by hand so you have to park, fumble with the relevant controls, then manually pull the roof to the favoured spot.

Electric Convertible Roof

See Manual Convertible Roof. In contrast, it operates via a motor and while the vehicle is in motion (if it is travelling slowly). The latter ensures there is no need to stop to position your roof.

Wind Deflector

The wind deflector is a removable screen that sits behind the seats in a convertible. Its purpose is to reduce how much wind, noise, and vibration enter the cabin once the roof is open.

Active Roll Bar

The active roll bar is a safety feature that emerges behind the seats if the car rolls. Along with the windscreen, it forms a safety zone to reduce the risk of hitting your head on the road.

Secondary Security Systems

Alarm

If a criminal tampers with the car, sensors trigger a loud siren that attracts attention and deters theft. The triggers include:

- forcing a door
- vibration
- movement in the cabin
- lifting the car to an angle that implies it is being towed.

Immobiliser

Without the immobiliser, thieves can easily manipulate the vehicle's ignition wires to make it start without its key fob. On this basis, the immobiliser must receive a deactivation code from the fob before it lets the engine have fuel. The immobiliser also incorporates a warning light on the dashboard that flashes once your vehicle is locked. Thieves then know it is not a soft target.

Entertainment and Connections

Analogue Radio

The analogue radio receives national and local broadcasts on traditional frequencies that crackle if the reception is poor. FM (frequency modulation) and AM (amplitude modulation), for example.

Digital Radio

Digital radio enables you to listen to national and local broadcasts on more modern, typically clearer digital frequencies.

Cassette Player

Player that accepts a single, reel to reel audio tape.

Compact Disc Player (CD)

Accepts a single audio disc.

Compact Disc Changer

Stores several audio discs simultaneously.

Auxiliary Port (AUX)

The auxiliary port lets you connect external devices such as a phone via a 3.5 to 3.5 millimetre cable. Why bother? Because it might contain thousands of songs you can play through the car's larger, better quality speakers. Farewell compact discs.

Universal Serial Bus Port (USB)

See Auxiliary Port for insight. In contrast, you connect via a universal serial bus cable and can charge the device.

Bluetooth

Connect an external device such as a phone without a wire. Now:

- make calls via the car's speakers and microphone
- hear music stored in the device via the car's speakers.

Television

Receives national and local television broadcasts.

Digital Video Disc Player (DVD)

This system lives in a front headrest, the screen points at the rear passengers, and it plays video discs.

Steering Wheel Audio Controls

Steering wheel audio controls put a range of functions at your fingertips. You can change the radio station and turn up the volume, for starters. The benefit is that you keep your hands on the steering wheel rather than stretching to reach the dashboard.

Wireless Phone Charger

Charge your smartphone without a wire by placing it on a mat.

Boot Fittings

Parcel Shelf

The parcel shelf is a large, awkward, yet light component that conceals cargo in the boot and rises and falls with the tailgate. It can also be removed to make the boot larger. However, it is then hard to store elsewhere in the vehicle due to its size.

Retractable Load Cover

The retractable cover works like a horizontal roller blind and conceals luggage in the boot. On this basis – and in contrast to the parcel shelf – it moves by hand rather than alongside the tailgate. On the plus side, it is far smaller than the parcel shelf once retracted. This makes it easier to store elsewhere within the vehicle if you remove it to make extra space for luggage.

Variable Height Boot Floor

The variable height floor is a movable panel that splits the boot into horizontal sections. You might use the lower section for rarely required items such as spare bulbs. The higher section might better suit cargo that is only in your boot briefly.

Miscellaneous

Automatic Engine Stop and Start

This system switches the engine off while the vehicle is stationary. At a red light, for instance. Its job is to save fuel and reduce emissions. The engine restarts automatically as needed.

Air Suspension

Traditional suspension incorporates springs that expand and contract to absorb bumps in the road. Air suspension has bellows at each wheel that perform the same task. The advantage is that the ride is smoother and more luxurious. Furthermore, you can adjust its height to best suit the terrain. Perhaps raise it off road to reduce the risk of hitting logs, rocks, and other nasties.

Head-up Display

The head-up display projects key information on the windscreen such as your current speed, the legal limit, and instructions from the satellite navigation. There is then less need to take your eyes off the road to look at the dashboard.

Gear Shift Indicator

This system minimises fuel consumption and emissions so works on the premise that it is best to keep the engine revolutions low. Expect a message on your dashboard that says when to change gear.

Fatigue Monitor

Are you finding it hard to steer properly? Is the vehicle wandering all over the road? If so, the fatigue monitor assumes the cause is a lack of sleep. It then suggests you stop and rest.

Virtual Cockpit

The virtual cockpit is a colour screen that replaces the instrument cluster that traditionally sits behind the steering wheel. It incorporates the speedometer, for starters. It also enables you to choose what information is shown (and how). You might prefer the satellite navigation to be the most dominant feature. Or would you rather have a big rev counter?

Trip Computer

The trip computer reveals various facts. Highlights include:

- average speed
- average fuel consumption
- current fuel consumption
- length of journey
- how many miles before the fuel is expired

Handling Control System

The handling control system optimises the response of the vehicle to suit your preferences and/or the conditions. Its modes include:

- comfort
- sport
- sport plus.

Perhaps you favour a sporty feel over comfort. Choose sport plus, then. Compared to the tamer settings it makes the:

- steering sharper
- suspension firmer
- automatic transmission more responsive
- traction control less likely to intervene.

Voice Recognition

Allows you to control a range of systems by voice command.

12 Volt Power Socket

Charges a phone, tablet, or other electrical item.

Router

The router creates a wi-fi network that keeps your smartphone, tablet, and laptop on the internet.

Satellite Navigation

Satellite navigation confirms how to get to your destination. The instructions come via voice command and a digital map. In addition, if there is congestion on the planned route it can divert you accordingly. Also expect points of interest. For example, the system knows how to find fuel, food, and hotels.

Traffic Sign Assist

As you pass a traffic sign this system sees it via a camera. A pictorial representation - not a photograph - then appears on the dashboard. It is handy if you forget the speed limit.

Made in the USA
Coppell, TX
04 October 2022